~ I LOVE TO YOU ~

~ I LOVE TO YOU ~

Sketch for a Felicity Within History

Luce Irigaray

Translated by Alison Martin

Routledge
New York and London

Published in 1996 by

Routledge
29 West 35th Street
New York, NY 10001

Published in Great Britain by
Routledge
11 New Fetter Lane
London EC4P 4EE

Design: David Thorne
Printed in the United States of America on acid-free paper.

Library of Congress Cataloging-in-Publication Data
  Irigaray, Luce.
  [J'aime à toi.   English]
I love to you: sketch for a felicity within history / Luce Irigaray: translated by
Alison Martin.
  p.   cm.
  Includes bibliographical references and index.
  ISBN 0-415-90732-2 (cl) — ISBN 0-415-90733-0 (pbk)
  1. Intersubjectivity.   2. Femininity (Philosophy)   3. Feminist theory.

B824.18.I7513   1995   94-13218
128—dc20   CIP

~

FOR RENZO IMBENI

~

~ CONTENTS ~

~ PROLOGUE ~

We met in Bologna, on May 30th, 1989, in San Donato, the reddest quarter of a very red city. It was during the election of Renzo Imbeni, the town's mayor, to the European Parliament. The invitation said the theme of the debate would be "New Rights in Europe," an appropriate theme given the tradition of the University of Bologna, which is famous for its law school. It was appropriate for me in that I believe priority should be given to the democratic objective of a jurisdiction that accords with the identity of real persons: men and women.

Going to this debate nevertheless presented me with a problem. The organizer was a man involved in mixed-sex politics, and the invitation was for a public meeting with a man. While the arrangements of a situation like this were in line with my own intentions, the question remained: how could I avoid surprising or offending the prominent female figures of that same party? So I informed the women national representatives in advance of the meeting. Such an outcry ensued that I thought it would be impossible to quell the surge of feeling this provoked. There were suspicions of assimilation by men, demands for me to appear at an additional women-only meeting, and a desire for the main meeting to be chaired by women. On this occasion, a gesture of recognition of female authority thus became a source of conflict and tension, leading to difficulties and a pointless waste of energy. Reactions such as these, where entrenched critiques and demands win out over an assessment of the facts and the issues, affirmed my belief in the need for objective laws to organize relations among women, and between women and men.[1]

The need is a particularly pressing one for women. In the absence of civil laws positively defining their real rights and duties, the only criteria women have to refer to are subjective ones. At best then, their laws or commandments are based on the say-so or opinion of a few women, which others adopt in the belief that it represents the/their truth, and because they are submitting to an authority that has been more or less consciously recognized, perhaps even by democratic vote.

But as long as there are no laws or rules which all women—and all men—may refer to and invoke when making their decisions, there can be no democracy, however attractive the immediate allegiance of a collectivity to a proposition may be. Anything put to the vote at a conference generally only concerns those present, a few militant women who have even gone so far as to state openly that their politics is based on egotism—a partially justifiable stance when compared with the policies of the state apparatus or of those pretending to complex considerations. And yet, by basing their politics on themselves, on their needs and desires (real or imagined as they may be), and not on those of all women, these practitioners of direct democracy or egological feminism in fact resubmit women as a whole to existing legislation. By showing no concern for the rights all women need—including the young girls of today and tomorrow, and women of other cultures—the decisions of such groups unnecessarily perpetuate (even accentuate through misunderstanding) injustice against the female gender. What is more, as they lack a positive definition of their gender and the objective qualities which give it an individual and collective content, these female minorities are very often formed in opposition to the other gender and from refusal of a mixed-sex culture. But this negative does not suffice to determine a valid judgment or a just community. It is merely the obvious counterpart to the exclusion of women by men— which in our era is not strikingly apparent due to the fact that customs are taken to be the norm or collective will.

Revenge is not an honorable historical or political tool. Aside from the fact that it divides what should operate as a non-oppositional dialectic it gives rise to conflicts and wars. And I would put this objection to Hegel before all others: wars are irrational and futile. Aside from its futility, the war of the sexes is impossible because of the love between man and woman, men and women, a love that has yet to be sublimated and which, if it were, would render war as an answer quite ridiculous.

Of course, how can we distance ourselves from or fail to applaud alliances among women if they advance the cause of justice for all women, for the whole of humanity? I myself wanted and participated in such allegiances over a number of years, while at the same time not forgetting the horizon of sexual difference corresponding to my inten- tion. The between-women sociality whose objective is the development of a homo-sexual sentiment without the creation of objective media- tions useful for all women and for relations between women and men does not serve the cause of the female gender but merely that of a minority of women—whose intentions are restricted and partial (although they do not acknowledge them). These women are still in a state of natural immediacy or unhappy consciousness, the traditional lot of the female gender. Consequently, they confuse their unmediated will with the model of law or the way to happiness for all women— indeed, for all women and men.

The argument that History progresses slowly, that women have only recently begun to make their mark, that they have been exploited for centuries and are still generally impoverished can no longer be put forward without qualification. Certain women are already making quite concerted efforts to aim for and make use of power, media power included, which often does nothing to help those exploited women whom they use to excuse their actions and whose awareness they jeopardize. As for History, things evolve both very slowly and very quickly at the same time. The important thing is to assist them to become, or to return in a direction that is just and fecund. And that means we must avoid fueling the growing mood of protest at the expense of recognizing not only debts but also, and more importantly, persons and truths.

Too many disagreements between women are nowadays perpetuated by the lack of objective determinations proper to the female gender. Perhaps it is necessary for a gender to learn to oppose itself but it is a shame that this opposition is still not worked through by each woman, or at least every feminist, within herself and that she continues to project her contradictions onto other women. It is disappointing, too, that instead of a real debate among women we have a genealogical division of roles that side-steps the labor of the negative amongst them. Hence, some women have defined themselves as the daughters of their theoretical and political elders, usually without consulting them, and they extract one aspect and one aspect alone from their work (conveniently allotted to the past), which they use as a focus for a being and a becoming for themselves and among themselves that is too exclusively positive. It is significant that, in the process, these "daughters" have distanced their "adopted mothers" from the sisterly alliance—like the sons of the primitive horde Freud describes?—and even this they seem to have renounced, despite the fact that it is sisterhood which has achieved the major theoretical and practical gains for women's liberation, and that it is both more spiritual and more revolutionary.

No doubt it is better to acclaim one aspect of an *oeuvre* than none at all, better to support female genealogy than to eradicate it, but the gesture remains an ambiguous one all the same because it runs the risk of erasing a path that for many is much freer and more accessible, a path more truthful because more real, dialectical and open to the future, as well as more democratic.

For such a development to come about requires more than the attainment of the immediate needs and desires of a woman, nor will it do to simply help her obtain the object she hopes for, even if it is an intellectual one. It is, rather, a question of awakening her to an identity and to rights and responsibilities corresponding to her gender. What women need most are mediations and means of distancing. Immediacy is their traditional task—associated with a purely abstract duty—but it places them back under the spiritual authority of men. And so to grant a woman what she wants without teaching her the detour of mediation boils down to behaving like a patriarch, against her interests.

Remaining within affectivity in relations among women also risks ensnaring their freedom in an attraction that exiles them from a return to themselves and distances them from the construction of a specific will and history. Women are often shown more esteem by being accorded a consciousness proper in them in private and public life, and mediations that enable them to exercise it, than by an immediate sensible love that, for want of a culture of difference, is in many respects delusive, alienating, and utopian. There is no need to present women with glowing promises of a new dawn for relations limited to within their own gender! That new dawn is not really imminent, as the doctrinaires of homo-sexuality are well aware. Yet, being closer to the tendencies of our tradition concerning relations between women and men,[2] they actually do far less to upset existing institutions and dogmas than would a real change in the respective status of the female and male genders. It is hardly surprising, therefore, that they might enjoy the actual support, either openly or indirectly, of authorities that at the same time refuse to bring in laws appropriate to female identity. Haven't these powers been structured, consciously or not, by homo-sexuality for centuries? An organization that is basically the same kind as their own and parallels it is barely a challenge to them compared with a fundamental reformulation of the principles of their economy. To demand a right to subjectivity and to freedom for women without defining the objective rights of the female gender seems an illusory solution belonging to the historic hierarchy between the sexes, and could even subject women to the authority of empty statements promulgated in an egological blindness confused with the collective good. And need I reiterate in this respect that being numerous is not the same as being democratic?

In order to express a real intention and not a superficial will, women must resolve the opposition between the subjective and objective with respect to the female gender's identity, particularly its historical identity.

The difficulties of taking such a step mean we need to establish objective categories and defenses that will open up the possibility of individual and collective development for women. Civil rights are the ones that can be defined in the most speedy and peaceful manner. This course of action can be realized within the framework of mixed-sex politics.

It was this objective that I wished to present to those women and men who had gathered at San Donato on May 30th, 1989. It was fitting given the invitation I had received and also given what I was able to put forward and support at a political meeting called for the purpose of electing a man from the Italian Communist Party[3] to the European Parliament. I was keeping faith with my identity and my task. I was helping him in his becoming, entrusting him with my own, ours, ours as women, to the extent that it can actually be formulated in rights which are vital for us.[4]

I did not know my interlocutor very well. He had publicly acknowledged me after I had spoken at his Party's 18th Congress. But, at the time, I did not realize the significance of that gesture.

And so I found myself in a situation that was new for me, with someone I did not know, and I had to speak, listen and respond in another language. But I wanted to take such a political step. I had no reason to be suspicious. And I had set as my goal a future fit for living.

I entered a packed hall. There were his people; there were my supporters. His people, adults and children, were certainly more organized than those who might be coming to hear me or reject me. His tribe already resembled a community; my crowd was only full of expectation, eagerness, impatience to hear and judge. His people were, on the whole, already enriched; my followers were still impoverished, though not without arrogance on occasion. He was installed in a city with his own; I incited individual awakenings or still nameless and homeless collective movements. He was in charge of citizens, many of whom were his associates, since he was their elected leader; I was addressing insurgents, radical spirits, reckless souls. He was surrounded by friends; I knew very few who were able to rally around me.

But things are not that simple. And there are times when the need for whatever already exists has partially exhausted itself, when what must emerge finds no place to express itself. Should such a space open up, then often the rebels make prophecies while respectable citizens cling to the realities and facts of a version of ordinary life that leaves us with no possibility of a future.

Nevertheless, that night, a miracle took place. We talked; we talked to each other: he and I, his citizens and my insurgents. Between us, each and every woman and man, there were truths, questions, passions, fidelities, words. We stayed together exchanging our views for at least three hours.

I changed the protocol of the meeting almost from the outset. Both he and I were to have answered written questions. But I did not want to have gone there without really meeting the men and women with whom I was speaking. I wished to see them, to hear their voices, to get physically close to them, too. Isn't writing made for long-distance dealings? For the far-off? For absence? Made up of words that are already partially abstract and bereft of flesh? Had I gone that far in order to read written questions? And, while his citizens had specific things to ask him, what could those who were there to listen to me expect from me? Certainly nothing in particular. I was in no position to grant them anything whatsoever, except for my presence, a few words, a subjective and objective representation of the right to exist.

This kind of need or desire cannot be met by the formal nature of the written question. Was it not quite an achievement itself to ensure that the speakers remain calm, that they did not overrun the time allotted to each person in a packed hall, and that they all retained their self-respect and respect for others?

There was another reason for this change in protocol. It was to be a meeting of women and men. The issue at stake was a political one. It concerned the rights necessary for the construction of Europe. Was not the first right women had to obtain that night the right to have their say? At the level of already existing rights, we could only battle in a relatively formal manner in this context: the misunderstandings were too fundamental, too historically entrenched, even among most of those on the left. On the other hand, it was possible to suggest there and then a fairly unusual democratic gesture: to invite anyone who wished or dared to speak to do so. To help everyone, women and men, to be involved, I wanted us to alternate between a question from a woman and a question from a man, and if possible, each to be addressed in turn to the man and then the woman on the podium. The advantage of this way of proceeding, which I have practiced for some years, is that it helps each gender to express itself in front of the other and starts to reveal the reality and fecundity of sexual difference.

The debate thus took place orally and was staged differently from the way it was originally planned. This provoked a bit of a stir. Men and women involved in party politics are less accustomed to such improvisations than I am, and at first some could only see a sort of intellectual capriciousness in my behavior. Yet, although this bothered the organizers and they showed that they were not particularly happy with it, Renzo Imbeni was not at all troubled by this disruption to the protocol and calmly supported my position.

That attitude was right politically. It was important to show both sexes that a cultural revolution is still possible, that it may be realized nonviolently and that, in our era, its most fecund intention lies primarily in the relations between women and men, between the legacy of 1968 and the tradition of a respected and cultured party of the left. While it would be pertinent to do this almost anywhere, it was especially apt in Bologna because of the student blood spilt in that city, for which the Italian Communist Party was allegedly in part responsible. I was aware of this factor. He too, no doubt.

By his reaction, he thus appeared to me as a man worthy of trust, quick to comprehend and clear-thinking, free from the defensiveness and inflexibility of a particular party line.

What also struck me and helped me, right from the beginning to the end of that debate, was how sound and fair he was in the way he carried himself. His attitude was nothing like that of a powerful patriarch, ruling over his land and men, but rather that of a fair and attentive man. If I was unable to follow all that he said because of the language difference and the tension due to the unusual and critical nature of this encounter, he listened carefully to what I was saying, to the precise translation of it—in fact, to everything that was exchanged—and he agreed or made his objections frankly and resolutely. This judiciousness and integrity took me by surprise at first. Added to that is his recognition of the other, which, doubtless to say, goes along with his sense of equity and the necessary criteria and concern he has for objectivity. He recognizes the other as what he or she already is and gives him or her the right or chance to exist. A little later on, something else caught my attention: his readiness to listen and the intelligence of his response.

I appreciate these qualities and I try to behave that way myself. They can only really be exercised and especially appear for what they are in reciprocity. They were possible that night at San Donato. Mutual respect occurred between us that few noticed, perhaps, but which was really there, and still is. We did not, for all that, renounce our own selves; otherwise the outcome would not have been as it was. We were two: a man and a woman speaking in accordance with our identity, our conscience, our cultural heritage, and even our sensibility.

Something like this is sufficiently rare to have made quite an impression in several respects.

I think the way it turned out was, in different ways, novel for both of us. Whether it entailed, entails, a sense of fecundity for him, I cannot say. He did say, to me and to others, that this debate had been an important one. In France, I sometimes read about his public statements in his Party's daily newspaper. From what I can glean of his proposals from the journalists' accounts, I believe I agree with them: a concrete democratic practice, control of the city to be given over to its citizens, a firm handling of underworld attacks and violence, the protection of nature, a concern for persons' rights, respect for cultural inheritance, of feminism especially, non-concessionary dialogue with Church representatives, prudence in speech, among others.

To be sure, a reality divides us, at least in part. He deals with the already possible; I defend the impossible. According to the press report on our meeting in Bologna, he accused me of asking the impossible. But am I actually allowed to do otherwise? Is not what is offered me already within a horizon that annihilates my identity and my will? Besides, I am offered very little. Since the publication of *Speculum*,[5] I have been defending the right to express myself particularly among male and female students, a right that, along with the right to do research, I am usually refused. I certainly seem to draw crowds, but I have been offered no context where I might consolidate the outcome of such meetings for the present and the future. I entrust the fecundity of my words to others, but they are not always properly understood and what remains of them bears only a slight resemblance to the intention behind them.

I am, therefore, a political militant for the impossible, which is not to say a utopian. Rather, I want what is yet to be as the only possibility of a future.

Perhaps Renzo Imbeni felt the urgency of this need for the impossible during our debate in San Donato. When I hear of what he is achieving, it seems to me he is shifting the boundaries between the possible and the impossible. Isn't this now our only chance? Be that as it may, he displaces these limits on the basis of an already existing framework. In his own way, he realizes a peaceful revolution in the context in which he finds himself. From what I know of all this, I have no regrets at being involved in his election to the European Parliament and I still expect him to support the project of a civil jurisdiction that makes possible national and international cohabitation between men and women.

As for the fecundity of this event, I am able to speak for myself and of what I can perceive thus far. Fecundity does not always take shape in the way we imagined it would. Those faithful (?) to me are angry at my working with a mixed-sex political group; his Party is experiencing a revolution. For months now, the world has been at war or is undergoing major upheavals.

And yet, at our meeting, there were the elements for a future whose horizon so often seems grim. There were decisive contributions concerning what lies beyond the fallen Marxist regimes. There was hope in a rationality, civility, culture and love that remain to be built between women and women. I would like to expand upon one aspect of this, even though I have to do it from a distance, hence, in writing, even though I have returned to inhabiting solitude for the moment whereas my aspiration would be to achieve things together, intelligently and affectionately. While he goes from city to city, from one conference to another, I am often to be found in the countryside, meditating. Perhaps I needed this time of withdrawal in order to understand, this return to what goes back the furthest in my life and my tradition in order to set off again one day, or maybe not, among humans. I like nature, so a retreat of this kind is not a burden for me. I am just surprised that I have given so much and gained so little in return: not only gratitude but recognition, too. Is this merely a question of what inevitably happens to thought? To a woman's thought? A question of the relation between these two? Of ill-being in the world which started I know not when exactly nor how long it will last? In any case, there is in this a lack of justice and harmony which causes a good deal of futile conflict, sluggishness, and hesitation. My vital rhythm does not always enable me to cope with so much procrastination, misunderstanding, and tardiness. Fortunately, I walk, I contemplate, I think, I write.

It is in the form of a book, then, that the outcome of the debate at San Donato will first manifest itself. A book concerning the encounter between woman and man, women and men. An encounter characterized by belonging to a sexed nature to which it is proper to be faithful; by the need for rights to incarnate this nature with respect; by the need for the recognition of another who will never be mine; by the importance of an absolute silence in order to hear this other; by the quest for new words which will make this alliance possible without reducing the other to an item of property; by the reinterpretation of notable figures or events in our tradition in terms of that horizon; by turning the negative, that is, the limit of one gender in relation to the other, into a possibility of love and of creation. The epilogue outlines the need for a new alliance between the female and male genders.

It was his political children who first asked me to speak of love and happiness, a gesture that seems to suggest the promise of a future.

The first version of the introduction to this volume was thus written for the girls and boys of the F.G.C.I.,[6] which he led before becoming mayor of Bologna. Twice did the young people of the F.G.C.I. ask me to talk to them. First, at their national conference in Modena, July, 1989. The proposed theme was "The right to life and happiness." And then, as part of the national *Unità* festival in Genoa, in September of that same year. The proposed title was "A man, a woman, love." I turned this into "Love between us," emphasizing the private and public relation between the genders rather than their juxtaposition. This choice also enabled me to move from the singular to the plural more easily.

In this text, I go back to Marx's *oeuvre* in order to criticize the inadequacy of its theory and practice as regards alienation in sexual difference. It is by going back to Hegel, and his conception of love as labor, that I take up the analysis of the exploitation of both woman and man alike in our familial-patriarchal culture. I put forward a different division of the nature-culture poles between male and female genders as well as an alliance between them that is no longer necessarily dependent upon the family and its objectives. This new alliance would range from the most private aspects of our lives to our most structured political institutions, whether national or international. Sometimes it is easier to establish this in the public realm than in simple subjective attraction because objectivity facilitates recognition and a pact between woman and man, women and men. The debate in Bologna was one example of this, rare no doubt, but it did really happen. Therefore such things are possible and could perhaps be generalized. Furthermore, such a method of exchange creates a distance between sensible immediacy and the passage to the universal, a distance that allows the former to be thought.

This I started to do at the request of the girls and boys of the F.G.C.I. I continued to do so with a course held at the International College of Philosophy in Paris from the beginning of March to the end of May, 1991.[7] In that case, too, the request came from students, both foreign and French. I had thought I would spend a year reflecting in order to develop this new dimension of my work in writing. But owing to the insistence of a few I was persuaded to come out of my solitude, although without giving up on my plans to reflect. I have thus continued to meditate, both in writing and orally, upon the labor that love represents in sexual difference.

Taking into consideration those young women and men who invited me to communicate something of this to them, this first written presentation will be briefer and more accessible than initially foreseen.

There are three interwoven intentions: the theoretical and practical furtherance of my work, a critical reading of Hegel, and fidelity to what happened at San Donato. All of these intentions certainly issue from the same will, but this will has undergone a strange conversion, or better yet, incarnation, realization, in the last few months.

For quite some time, but on a more continuous basis since 1981, I have been looking at Hegel's work. The experience of the negative, which I found quite intense that particular year, seemed painful to me, particularly since the use of this process aimed at an assumption towards absolute spirit was ethically impossible for me. What I knew of the negative was the practice and the effects of moderation, measuredness, renunciation, a certain cultivation of personal sensibility, but it lacked any real return either in myself or for myself. As for an absolute in-itself or for-itself, I could see their limitations only too well to believe in them and desire them.

The asceticism of the negative thus seemed necessary to me but more out of consideration for the other and from collective good sense than as a process of consciousness that would lead me to a more accomplished spirituality. Let us say that this negative created a space for potential meeting or listening within me.

If neither absolute spirit nor the traditional Western monotheistic God seem to be the paths of a becoming, how can we ensure that the negative does not entail martyrdom? There remain the resources of the natural universe with which the cultivation of sensibility opens up more subtle and gratifying exchanges. That is why there is so much grief following a disaster like the one at Chernobyl, and, more generally, so much suffering caused by man's technological domination of nature.

However, the natural universe is still not the human universe. It is more and less than that. The meeting at San Donato led me to discover that the negative can mean access to the other of sexual difference and thereby become happiness without being annihilating in the process. Hegel knew nothing of a negative like that. His negative is still the mastery of consciousness (historically male), over nature and human kind. The negative in sexual difference means an acceptance of the limits of my gender and recognition of the irreducibility of the other. It cannot be overcome, but it gives a positive access—neither instinctual nor drive-related—to the other.

Such a conception of the negative provides the underlying thread for this work on recognition and love between woman and man, women and men, in dual and community relations. It facilitates a cultivation of the sexed dimension, thus far left to an empiricism without a civil culture or an ethics. The individual cultivation of sexed subjectivity is destroyed by divine commandments, existing marriage laws, and a hierarchy of social power tied to the prevalence of genealogical familial authority; the latter are what subject people to imperatives (which may be necessary due to the lack of cultivation of the sexual, but which are relatively arbitrarily imposed all the same), to uninterpreted historical determinations, to an unjust division of dignity and labor between the genders, and to a loss of identity in laws and cultural mechanisms abstracted from natural and generic reality.

With this new elaboration of the negative, it may be possible for another era of human becoming and its incarnation in History to open up. It would be a development of the human realized on the basis of what really exists: women and men, and without any additional fabrications which might alienate and annihilate what should be cultivated. Without producing unnecessary luxury, then, be it economic or cultural. The proliferation of possessions and knowledge is gradually burying us in objects or secondary realities; surrounded by them we become incapable of distinguishing the most useful from the most alienating.

To return to ourselves as living beings who are engendered and not fabricated is a vital and ethical need of paramount importance. If we want to go on living and governing our creations, we must make sure we do this.

The fall of the Marxist regimes is also an invitation to do so. The communist regimes made many mistakes, of course, but it would be better to ask ourselves where they went wrong rather than decide upon revenge or draw conclusions as to the cyclical character of History. Attaching prime importance to material goods, using violence as an arm of power, giving insufficient consideration to the law of persons and especially the different rights required by women and men who make up social communities—these seem to be areas of injustice and alienation that remain unresolved in Marxist and democratic regimes.

Rather than regressing to the simple authority of a religion—which one?—or blindly submitting to the rule of money, capital, and methods of production that are competitive and irresponsible, we can pursue an *oeuvre* of justice and culture by elaborating a real civil culture of persons and of the subjective and objective relations between them.

We must also think about constructing our happiness.

To say that felicity will come from owning goods or that happiness is to be found in the beyond, this earth being just an exile, is to make two illusory promises.

Happiness must be built by us here and now on earth, where we live, a happiness comprising a carnal, sensible and spiritual dimension in the love between women and men, woman and man, which cannot be subordinated to reproduction, to the acquisition or accumulation of property, to a hypothetical human or divine authority. The realization of happiness in us and between us is our primary cultural obligation. It is not an easy task to realize. It is constantly avoided, replaced by secondary and basically futile activities. Becoming happy implies liberating human subjectivity from the ignorance, oppression and the lack of culture that weighs so heavily upon this essential dimension of existence: sexual difference.

In this respect, to become equal is to be unfaithful to the task of incarnating our happiness as living women and men. Equality neutralizes that dimension of the negative which opens up an access to the alliance between the genders. This avatar of a partly nihilistic philosophy, religion and Marxism weighs on our consciousness. A certain Western interpretation of Buddhism or Brahmanism may throw them a life-line at the eleventh hour. We can only perish from such abstract and disincarnated conceptions of spirit.

It remains the case that, among us, there are women and men who are still alive. And that from this meeting of living men and women, everything once more becomes possible, everything, including felicity within History.

At San Donato, there were living men and women. I did not get close to all of them. One of them, at least, I recognized.

So alive, faces light up around him. Alive, he saves a city from pollution and makes it a habitable place once again, one where air and wind can circulate, where we can hear and talk to one another once again. Alive, he is daring and unsubmissive, but he does have respect, both for nature and for others. He is innovative in safeguarding what is worth keeping of the *oeuvre* of our tradition. He progresses without accumulating; he shares without complacence. He is prudent and daring. He only makes promises he can keep. It is possible to have faith in him. One can take from him without renouncing one's self.

You are probably thinking that I must be blinded by some sort of passion for him, some projection onto him? I can only say that these praises are commonplace in all the squares, restaurants or public places in his city. Even without knowing it, his citizens sing his praises, since they exhibit a joyfulness not found in many cities. Some rather unreceptive minds, or those too embittered to yet be capable of admiration, claim that gastronomic pleasures alone make the people of Bologna happy. I believe that a soul watching over them with attentiveness and serenity is just as important.

But, by revealing so much about him, don't we risk forcing his reserve? Don't we risk paralyzing with the glory of words what moves within the humility of a body? Yet, by attesting to the qualities of the other, to what he communicates, we also do justice.

And shouldn't there still be thanks for the one who gives you cause for praise? For if we can no longer praise, haven't we lost all inspiration? And therefore life?

Let no one take offense at this unique recognition. Such an experience was—is?—necessary for me to be able to perceive what there is of the negative in sexual difference. Yet this gesture cannot be to the detriment of any other since its uniqueness forces me more than ever to respect everyone, whether they be woman or man.

Notes

1. I had already given and published a paper on this matter at the *Unità* festival in Florence in 1988, "Droits et devoirs civils pour les deux sexes," published in French in *Le Temps de la différence*, Biblioessais, 1989. English trans. forthcoming, Karen Montin, Athlone Press.

2. See my *Speculum, De l'autre femme* (Paris: Minuit, 1976), trans. Gillian C. Gill, *Speculum of the Other Woman* (Ithaca: Cornell University Press, 1985), with particular reference to the guiding principle of its analysis and interpretation of our tradition as a civilization founded upon self-identity, the love and thought of the same, and the privileging of the specular and of homo-sexuality in what is given to be the symbolic order.

3. For most of its members, the Italian Communist Party has become the Democratic Left.

4. The content of my introduction to this debate may be found in the reply to questions 3 and 4 in "*Pourquoi définir des droits sexués*," *Je, tu, nous* (Grasset, 1990), trans. "Why define sexed rights?" in, *Je, Tu, Nous, Toward a Culture of Difference*, trans. Alison Martin, Routledge, 1993. A synthesis of these ideas is given in the conclusion to this volume, *"Love: Between Passion and Civility."*

5. *Speculum, De l'autre femme*, op. cit.

6. The Italian Federation of Young Communists.

7. A place established with the aim of providing a context in which those denied access to mainstream institutions may express themselves. I have taught there since the 1988–89 academic year.

~ I ~

Introducing: Love Between Us

Marx defined the origin of man's exploitation of man as man's exploitation of woman and asserted that the most basic human exploitation lies in the division of labor between man and woman. Why didn't he devote his life to solving the problem of this exploitation? He perceived the root of all evil but he did not treat it as such. Why not? The reason, to some extent, lies in Hegel's writings, especially in those sections where he deals with love, Hegel being the only Western philosopher to have approached the question of love as labor.

It is, therefore, entirely appropriate for a woman philosopher to start speaking of love. It results from the need to think and practice what Marxist theory and practice have thus far ignored, giving rise to merely piecemeal economic and cultural developments which can no longer satisfy us. To cite just three examples or symptoms of these: the fate of the earth as a natural resource, problems to do with women's liberation, and the world-wide cultural crisis as exemplified by the student revolts that have arisen, and re-arisen in France and elsewhere since '68. What is more, it is from this same crucible of cultural revolution that various struggles—students, feminists of difference, ecological movements—have erupted and re-erupted in our countries. Their concerns live on, concerns often suppressed by powers blind to their objectives or by militants who barely understand the profundity and radical nature of what is at stake in these struggles. For it is not a matter of changing this or that within a horizon already defined as human culture. It is a question of changing the horizon itself—of understanding that our interpretation of human identity is both theoretically and practically wrong.

Analyzing the relations between men and women can help us to change this situation. If we fail to question what cries out to be radically questioned, we lapse or relapse into an infinite number of secondary ethical tasks, as Hegel wrote when discussing the failing that has marred our whole culture.[1] That failing concerns the lack of ethical relations between the sexes. And those countless ethical tasks, which multiply in proportion to the complexity of our civilizations, do not accomplish the *oeuvre* to be carried out: to remove the exploitation that exists between the sexes so as to allow humanity to continue developing its History.

So I will return to Hegel to explain the reasons for this exploitation and to suggest how the situation might be remedied.

At several points in his *oeuvre*, and at several moments in his life, Hegel reflects on the question of love between the sexes which, notably, he analyzes as labor. How does Hegel define love between men and women? He defines it as it is still often practiced in our time, but also as it is defined by monotheistic, patriarchal religions, or, ostensibly at the other extreme, by theories of sexuality, like the Freudian one. He defines it, on the whole, as we still find ourselves accustomed and obliged to experience it, in private and in public. He defines it as it exists within patriarchal cultures, without managing to resolve the problem of the lack of spirit and ethics he observes. He also defines it in terms of his method. Which means that in order to overcome what he terms natural immediacy within the family Hegel turns to pairs of opposites. Hence he is forced to define man and woman as opposites and not as different. But isn't this just how male and female genders are still usually interpreted?

Man and woman are thus in opposition to one another in the labor of love, according to Hegel. This labor is analyzed within the family they form as a couple (of opposites). Beyond the family context, Hegel shows little concern for granting each gender its own identity, particularly a legal one, even though he states that the status of the human person depends upon his or her recognition by civil law. From his perspective, then, sexed law should pertain only to the family. There would be no sexed identity for the citizen.

This is still the case for us. There are still no civil rights proper to women and to men.[2] This is particularly true for women, since existing law is better suited to men than women inasmuch as men have been the model for citizenship for centuries, the adult female citizen being poorly defined by rights to equality that do not meet her needs. Strictly speaking, there is still no civil law in our era that makes human persons of men and women. As sexed persons, they remain in natural immediacy. And this means that real persons still have no rights, since there are only men and women; there are no neuter individuals. The rights of these abstract citizens are, to varying degrees, modeled upon or derived from religious rights and duties, in particular patriarchal ones. Hence the difficulty of distinguishing between these two domains. We do not as yet have civil law pertaining to real persons, concerning first of all women and men. For want of such laws, our sexuality lapses into a barbarity worse at times than that of animal society.

How then, for Hegel, are relations between woman and man organized within the family?[3] The woman is wife and mother. But, for her, this role is a function of an abstract duty. So she is not *this* woman, irreducible in her singularity, wife of *this* man, who is himself also irreducible, any more than she is *this* mother of *this* child or *these* children. She is only attributed that singularity from the perspective of the man, for whom she remains bound to natural immediacy. As far as she is concerned, she is a wife and mother inasmuch as these roles represent a task vis-à-vis the universal which she discharges by renouncing her singular desires.

Love, as Hegel writes of it, is therefore not possible on the part of the woman, because it is a labor of the universal, in the sense that she has to love man and child without loving *this* man or *this* child. She must

~

love man and child as generic representatives of the human species dominated by the male gender. She must love them as those who are able to realize the infinity of humankind (unconsciously assimilated to the masculine), at the expense of her own gender and her own relationship to infinity. In other words, a woman's love is defined as familial and civil duty. She has no right to singular love nor to love for herself. She is thus unable to love but is to be subjugated to love and reproduction. She has to be sacrificed and to sacrifice herself to this task, at the same time disappearing as this or that woman who is alive at the present time. And she must disappear as desire, too, unless it is abstract: the desire to be wife and mother. This self-effacement in a family-related role is her civil task. For the man, on the other hand, a woman's love represents the repose a citizen needs in the singularity of the home. He has to love *this* woman considered as singular nature, provided she stays bound to that singularity and provided he may pass over into it while remaining faithful to his relation to the universal.

For woman, therefore, the universal comes down to practical labor within the horizon of the universal delimited by man. Deprived of a relationship to the singularity of love, woman is also deprived of the possibility of a universal for herself. Love, for her, amounts to a duty—not a right—establishing her role within humankind where she appears as man's servant.

As for man, he yields to the singularity of love as a regression to natural immediacy. Love with a woman in his own home is rest, complementing his citizen's labor. As a citizen he is expected to renounce his sexed singularity in order to realize a universal task in the service of the community. In the name of this alleged universality, he apparently has the right and duty to represent the entire human species in public life.

Love, for the man, is thus a permissible lapse into natural immediacy. His wife or some other woman is duty bound to grant him this regression given the arduous labor of the universal for which he is responsible on the outside. Yet she also has to send him back to this task, to distance him from herself, to ceaselessly engender him as artisan of the universal spirit. Redemption for the man's fall into singularity lies in his ensuing capacity to resume his labor as a citizen, in the child, whose conception prevents

~

the man from possessing his *jouissance* as his own, as well as in the accumulation of possessions (ostensibly jointly owned by both sexes), possessions that represent the for-itself of the union between man and woman in the family. The ultimate aim of love for the couple is, basically, the accumulation of family capital. For this reason, the family appears to be a privileged locus for constituting property.

Evidently, the self-renunciation in love demanded of woman is connected to man's loss of identity as a citizen. The woman is forced to comply with the lack of forms and norms of a male desire that may very well be defined against incest, against the other who is non-possessable in her singularity—the mother—but is not named as male desire, except when theorized as willing enslavement to death.

In fact, for centuries in the West marriage as an institution has bound women to a universal duty for the sake of the development of man's spirit in the community, and bound men to a regression to the natural to ensure that the interests of the State are served in other respects. Real marriages do not exist to the extent that two legally-defined sexed persons do not exist. Both are enslaved to the State, to religion, to the accumulation of property. What's more, this absence of two in the couple forces the intervention of other limits deriving from the labor of the negative on man's terms: death as the rallying place of sensible desires, the real or symbolic dissolution of the citizen in the community, and enslavement to property or capital.

This division of tasks between home and the public realm could not be sustained without depriving woman of a relationship to the singular in love and of the singularity necessary for her relationship to the universal. The home—the couple or family—should be a locus for the singular and universal for both sexes, as should the life of a citizen as well. This means that the order of cultural identity, not only natural identity, must exist within the couple, the family, and the State. Without a cultural identity suited to the natural identity of each sex, nature and the universal are parted, like heaven and earth; with an infinite distance between them, they marry no more. This division of tasks between heaven and earth, suffering and labor here below, recompense and felicity in the beyond, begins at a period in our culture that is described in mythology and inscribed into philosophy and theology (and also separated, from that time on, which is not the case, for instance, in most traditions of the Far East).

Such a conception of the world is actually totally foreign to that of other cultures in which the body is spiritualized as body and the earth as earth, the celestial being the manifestation of our degree of spirituality here and now. I am thinking of certain traditions of yoga that I know something of, cultures where the body is cultivated as body, not only just in that muscular-athletic competitive-aggressive way we know only too well and which is not at all beneficial to us. In these traditions, the body is cultivated to become both more spiritual and more carnal at the same time. A range of movements and nutritional practices, attentiveness to breath in respiration, respect for the rhythms of day and night, for the seasons and years as the calendar of the flesh, for the world and for History, the training of the senses for accurate, rewarding and concentrated perception—all these gradually bring the body to rebirth, to give birth to itself, carnally and spiritually, at each moment of every day. The body is thus no longer simply a body engendered by my parents; it is also the one I give back to myself. Likewise, immortality is no longer reserved for the beyond and the conditions for it cease to be determined by one who is other to me. Each woman and man acquires immortality by respecting life and its spiritualization. The universal—if this word can still be used here—consists in the fulfillment of life and not in submission to death as Hegel would have it. By training the senses in concentration we can integrate multiplicity and remedy the fragmentation associated with singularity and the distraction of desiring all that is perceived, encountered, or produced. There is no question, then, of renouncing the sensible, of sacrificing it to the universal, but rather it is cultivated to the point where it becomes spiritual energy. And so the Buddha's gazing at the flower is not an inattentive or predatory gaze, nor the decline of the speculative into flesh. It is both material and spiritual contemplation, furnishing thought with an already sublimated energy.

This contemplation is also a training in finding pleasure while respecting what does not belong to me. Indeed, Buddha contemplates the flower without picking it. He gazes at what is other to him without uprooting it. Moreover, what he is gazing at is not just anything—it is a flower, which perhaps offers us the best object for meditation upon the

~

24

appropriateness of form to matter.

Buddha's gazing at the flower might provide us with a model. So might the flower. Between us, we can train ourselves to be both contemplative regard and the beauty appropriate to our matter, the spiritual and carnal fulfillment of the forms of our body. Pursuing this simultaneously natural and spiritual meditation of a great Eastern sage, I'd say that a flower usually has a pleasant scent. It sways with the wind, without rigidity. It also evolves within itself; it grows, blossoms, grows back. Some of them, those I find most engaging, open with the rising sun and close up with the evening. There are flowers for every season. The most hardy among them, those least cultivated by man, come forth while preserving their roots; they are constantly moving between the appearance of their forms and the earth's resources. They survive bad weather and winters. These are the ones, perhaps, that might best serve us as a spiritual model.

Of course we are spirit, we have been told. But what is spirit if not the means for matter to emerge and endure in its proper form, its proper forms? What is spirit if it forces the body to comply with an abstract model that is unsuited to it? That spirit is already dead. An illusory ecstasy in the beyond. The capitalization of life in the hands of a few who demand this sacrifice of the majority. More especially, the capitalization of the living by a male culture which, in giving itself death as its sole horizon, oppresses the female.

Thus the master-slave dialectic occurs between the sexes, forcing woman to engender life to comply with the exigencies of a universal linked to death. This also forces woman to mother her children so as to subject them to the condition of being citizens abstracted from their singularity, severed from their unique identity, arising from their genealogical and historical conception and birth, adults or adolescents who are subsequently exposed to the risk of actual death for the sake of the *polis* or to a spiritual death for the sake of culture.

This is how woman herself becomes an agent of ambivalence in love, contrary to her singular desire. Raised for love, familiar with this inter-subjective dimension from the fact of having been born the daughter of a woman, she finds herself obliged to sacrifice this love, except as an abstract labor of *jouissance*, of having children, of motherhood. Where she was expecting to realize her identity, she finds only self-sacrifice. If a man is always able to find another woman, another singularity, to work towards accumulating property for the family or the community, to return to his citizenship, the woman is left with nothing other than the obligation to make herself available for intercourse, to suffer childbirth, to mother her children and her husband. Even the love between mother and daughter is forbidden in the sense that it reminds the daughter, the woman, of the singularity of the female gender she has to renounce, except as an abstract duty imposed upon her by a culture that is not hers and inappropriate for her. The girl's only reason for being is to become a wife and mother. In this respect, her mother represents this abstract role for her, as she does for the mother. They are two functionaries of the universal, a universal inappropriate to their singular nature, so forever foreign to one another. The daughter is the child of the universal in her mother.

With this erasure within the universal, or this sacrifice to the spirit, of the relationship between mother and daughter, there occurs the most extreme loss of human singularity. Humanity unconsciously persists in its crime, this abduction of the one from the other as a member of the female gender, without mourning its loss. We know from myth that it can bring about the sterility of the earth. By unraveling the enigma of our decadence, we might learn that it can entail the end of the human species sacrificed to an abstract universal: absolute spirit.

So how can we get way from such an abstract duty, from the sacrifice of sexed identity to a universal defined by man with death as its master, for want of having known how to let life flourish as the universal? How can we discover for ourselves, between ourselves, the singularity and universality of love as the natural and spiritual realization of human identity? It will come from the evolution, the revolution in the relations between man and woman, first and foremost in the couple, and before any question of the family. The changes to be made in mother-daughter relationships are connected to this transformation of relations between the two genders of the human species, requiring the transition to a culture which is not reducible to a single gender, nor reducible to a sexed dimension that is simply genealogical, and thus to patriarchy or matriarchy.

In concrete terms, this means that each woman will no longer love her lover as Man (in general), nor will each man love his lover as *a* woman (who can be replaced by another). The task of making the transition from the singular to the universal thus remains for each person in his or her own unique singularity, and especially for each sex in the both singular and universal relationship it maintains with itself and with the other sex. Each woman will, therefore, be for herself woman in the process of becoming, the model for herself as a woman and for the man whom she needs, just as he needs her, to ensure the transition from nature to culture. In other words, being born a woman requires a culture particular to this sex and this gender, which it is important for the woman to realize without renouncing her natural identity. She should not comply with a model of identity imposed upon her by anyone, neither her parents, her lover, her children, the State, religion or culture in general. That does not mean she can lapse into capriciousness, dispersion, the multiplicity of her desires, or a loss of identity. She should, quite the contrary, gather herself within herself in order to accomplish her gender's perfection for herself, for the man she loves, for her children, but equally for civil society, for the world of culture, for a definition of the universal corresponding to reality. With regard to this task, claiming to be equal to a man is a serious ethical mistake because by so doing woman contributes to the erasure of natural and spiritual reality in an abstract universal that serves only one master: death. Aside from her own suicide, she thus deprives man of the possibility of defining himself as man, that is as a naturally and spiritually sexed person. For each man must remain a man in the process of becoming. He himself has to accomplish the task of being *this* man he is by birth and a model of humanity, a model that is both corporeal and spiritual. It is not right for him to leave himself to the woman's cultural maternal care, especially as she, not being him, cannot take responsibility for him. He has to become man by himself, to grow without her and without opposing himself to her in the process. He must be capable of sublimating his instincts and drives himself, not only his partial drives but also his genital drives. Extolling the pre-oedipal as a liberation from the norm of genital sexuality entails all the caprice and immaturity of desire exercised to the detriment of becoming human as a genus, as two genders.

~

And to those who advocate the pre-oedipal against Freud the response is simple: the sublimation of the pre-genital is present in Freud's work, but not the sublimation of genitality which is reduced to reproduction.

Now, reproduction does not exhaust all drives of desire between the sexes. Hence, those drives that are a function of this attraction are neutralized and diverted to serve the interests of the family, the community and the State without being sublimated as intersubjective desire. In other words, male desire must become desire *for oneself* as man and *for the other* woman. Sexed desire, sexual desire, should not have its end, its effectivity, in the family as such, nor in the State, nor in religion, for then it perverts the truth and spirit of the community. Sexual desire demands a realization appropriate to its matter, its nature. This realization takes place in the body proper and in the couple that man forms with the other sex— woman. This couple forms the elementary social community. It is where sensible desire must become potentially universal culture, where the gender of the man and of the woman may become the model of male human kind or of female human kind while keeping to the singular task of being *this* man or *this* woman. In realizing the transition from nature to culture, from the singular to the universal, from sexual attraction to actualizing gender, the couple formed by the man and the woman ensures the salvation of the community and of nature, both together. It is not merely their pleasure which is at stake but the order of the becoming spirit of the entire community and the conservation of nature as macro- and microcosm, as human species and gender. The attraction between the sexes would thus not be left without a *for-itself*, which has become the child, family property or the service of a male culture or community dominated by death as guarantor of the universal. Sexual pleasure does not then blindly or cynically become social power of a patriarchal or matriarchal type exercised in the home or in public life. Nor would sexual desire be left uncultured, impulsive, turning the couple into a place of debauchery (a natural place, Hegel would say), an alternative to the order of citizenship. Desire and pleasure are then cultivated by and for each sex with the intention of accomplishing the perfection of its gender. The man trains his instincts and drives so as to become fully man and the woman does the same in order to accomplish the perfection of her gender. The man and the woman can thus form a human couple. In the couple sexuality finds its actualization, its realization, an *in-itself* and a *for-itself* corresponding to the poles needed for the perfect incarnation of every man and woman's humanity. This task is realized separately and together.

We know nothing of that dimension Hegel called the labor of love, or at least not any more. And we are prevented from doing so by the cultural order. We must interpret and go beyond this order in that it represents alienation from the human for both sexes and for humanity as a whole, alienation leading the human species to its loss. For love seems to remain a natural affliction, its only possible redemption being the spiritual authoritarianism of a community dominated by a patriarchal father. Of love, we know only the singularity of sensible desire bereft of a *for-itself*, the torments of attraction for the other, the weight of sinfulness and the price we pay for our redemption. We know about the loneliness of desire, the desperation of rejection or of wanting the impossible, the pathological derangements of the drives, the destitution of parting. We know, too, the passionate resurgence of desire for someone, a singular desire for the one feeling it but an inexpressible, ultimately irrational desire, with no language for the one who inspires it and thus an aspiration devoid of any possible reciprocity except for the blind and annihilating reciprocity this kind of mentality produces. We also know the shame of desire, its engulfment in the loss of identity, its chaos, its drug of disillusioned tomorrows. We still know nothing of the salvation love brings, individual and collective salvation.

For centuries in our cultures felicity has been presented to us as, at best, genealogical. It has been said that happiness is found in the family, the genealogically male family, the family in the strict or general sense, a family in which woman remains bound to nature and is given the task of letting the natural pass over into the universal by renouncing her own desire and her female identity. This beatitude may have had a meaning at one time in History. But was not that meaning already regressive in relation to other stages of culture? In any case, we need to realize History—or at least continue it—as the salvation of humanity comprised of men and women. That is our task. In accomplishing it, we are working for History's development by bringing about more justice, truth, and humanity in the world. This is the task for our time, (albeit one that may once again reestablish links with repressed, forgotten, or hidden traditions). It is a task for everyone. No one is beyond it, and it makes no one naturally a master or slave, poor or rich. We are all of us, men and women alike, sexed. Our principal task is to make the transition from nature to culture as sexed beings, to become women and men while remaining faithful to our gender. This task, which exists for all men and women, must not be confused with reproduction. That is a different task, which can only be done properly if the principal one is respected. Only women and men concerned to fulfill their gender, both carnally and spiritually, as a couple and in society, can engender children with dignity. Reproduction cannot be reduced to an order ensuing from an absent master or his omnipotent mediators. It must be the fruit of love cultivated between woman and man. Otherwise, it represents humanity's decline from its spiritual task and, more especially, the enslavement of woman to a natural identity in order to uphold a partial, unjust and abstract culture—a culture of human kind dominated by a masculinity that does not take itself to be a singular gender.

Engendering a child is to be understood by the same measure as the engendering of society, History and the universe. The child must be the natural and spiritual fruit of the labor of love within each couple at a given moment of world History. Engendering a child cannot be separated from the engendering of the natural and spiritual place into which she or he may be welcomed. Without this care, having children falls back into uncultured instinct. An act that becomes a failing which corrupts the whole of humanity.

Sanctified desire—to use Hegel's language—does not in his view consist in the engendering of children because they represent the *for-itself* of the *in-itself* of the parent's desire, a desire that is henceforth desire for death, but not sanctified in its natural substance. Nor does sanctified desire correspond to the joint ownership of family property, as Hegel (and plenty of others!) would have it, but can rather be understood as the transition for each gender from the natural to the spiritual, from nature to culture. And in that lies the couple's most saintly *oeuvre*: to spiritualize human kind through its sexed representatives, man and woman. For sexual desire is not satisfied by labor in general, it has its own labor to accomplish. It must be cultivated for its own development.

It has its end in itself. Sexual desire is not to be sacrificed to the labor of the community. This labor does not realize sexual desire, anyway. As the personal property of either one or the other sex it is impoverished. And it is wrong to suggest that the profit accrued from it to the family, in the form of cash or property or capital, can be a suitable payment for the expenditure of desire. For this so-called jointly-owned property, which is often acquired by the man and by means of the economy of his world, cannot correspond to an immediately spiritual possession, as Hegel writes, because it is an inanimate object and we are not commensurable to such an object. The object may perhaps be used for mediation, but such mediation is better suited to exchanges between men, women preferring intersubjective relations. Furthermore, using money as a means of mediation represents the loss or alienation of singularity in a universal abstracted from the natural without a suitable spiritualization of this natural nor a possible return to the self.

What can be a mediation between the sexes is to sample the other's substance insofar as it is already spiritual while remaining sensible. An act that seems impossible to Westerners who no longer know anything of love in its simultaneously corporeal and spiritual dimension. But by reading certain texts on yoga, for example, we can learn that spiritual substance does exist and is not experienced as a property exterior to the self. In other words, the interior or the interiority of a body is cultivated and is not to be reduced to the obscurity of the natural. Love as objectivity can be known as sexed love and the lovers may contemplate themselves and each other as the subjects and objects of love. Some Indian traditions are still very close to such a contemplation of the objectivity of love, which is subject to a rigorous corporeal and spiritual apprenticeship. In the tradition of yoga, for example, making love does not mean a return to a zero degree of tension but rather making energy circulate between *chakras* (nerve centers which are both physical and spiritual), between the lowest and highest *chakras*. Making love carnally in this way means cultivating your instincts together, making them pass from the *chakra* of the stomach to those of the heart, the throat, the head, using breath as mediation.

Love is not contemplated, then, in the child who is an other easy to produce sexually, and who represents the sacrifice of the lovers to genealogy. Love is contemplated in the lovers who love each other in a more or less accomplished way.

It seems that our culture, supported by morality, always tends to make us lapse to the most base level of love, especially by reducing the aim of love to reproduction. One act of intercourse is all that it takes to engender a child. Sublimating one's amorous energy is a far more subtle and sublime task. And blessed are those children freely conceived in the sublimated energy of the lovers. Blessed are the children of lovers spiritualized in their flesh. By birth they are already naturally spiritual since they were not conceived in love's degeneracy, the simple mix of semen and egg resulting from some more or less successful coupling. They are the children of a couple spiritual enough to share their treasure with a third, a treasure that is subjective and objective, natural and spiritual. They are the children love announces and awaits. They are the sons and daughters who find spiritual bodies to welcome them, to cradle them, nourish them, love them, talk to them, bodies that yet remain carnally vibrant and happy as well. They are the children of the word of their parents as much as they are the children of their flesh. The lovers' culture of sexuality is transmitted through their speech, even if it is silent gesture. For such children, the body, the house, the public realm, are all inhabitable places. One passes over into the other without imperative. Body, home and public domain are the *oeuvre* jointly constructed by men and women for today and for the future, and with respect for their ancestors. The objectivity of love in this case is no longer just the child or family or communal property but the natural and cultural world engendered by women and men at a given moment in History.

That is the task I set for us, the happiness I wish for us, for each and every woman and man. For today and tomorrow. For our loves, the political order we are part of, for nature and the entire universe. Love between us, women and men of this world, is what may save us still.

The word "companions" refers to those women and men who share not just bread but love, too. It is sometimes used for the lovers of the *Song of Songs*, the only erotic love hymn in the Bible. But the lovers of the *Song* are still divided between two genealogies or cultures: that of the mother for the woman, that of the King for the man. We have to see if we can be companions who marry and form alliances, instead of separating, being torn between genealogies, cultures, and the sexes. We are the ones who have to make this word designate a loving relationship, ranging from the most private aspects of our lives to a political ethics that refuses to sacrifice desire for death, power, or money.

Notes

1. In chapter VI of *The Phenomenology of Spirit*.
2. Tolerance of abortion (in those countries where there is tolerance) clearly does not constitute a real civil right. It is just the bare beginnings of such a right.
3. Refer particularly to *The Philosophy of Right*, *Philosophy of Spirit*, and *Natural Law*.

~ 2 ~

Human Nature is Two

The natural is at least two: male and female. All the speculation about overcoming the natural in the universal forgets that nature is not *one*. In order to go beyond—assuming this is necessary—we should make reality the point of departure: it is *two* (a *two* containing in turn secondary differences: smaller/larger, younger/older, for instance). The universal has been thought as *one*, thought on the basis of *one*. But this *one* does not exist.

If this *one* does not exist, limit is therefore inscribed in nature itself. Before the question of the need to surpass nature arises, it has to be made apparent that it is *two*. This *two* inscribes finitude in the natural itself. No one nature can claim to correspond to the whole of the natural. There is no "Nature" as a singular entity. In this sense, a kind of negative does exist in the natural. The negative is not a process of consciousness of which only man is capable. More to the point, if man does not take account of the limit inscribed in nature, his opposition to the natural does not accomplish the labor of the negative. It appropriates the natural and claims to overcome it by a consciousness subsequently determined by that natural naïveté: I am the whole.

Now no woman or man accomplishes the whole in herself or himself, neither of nature nor of consciousness. Confusing the part for the whole taints the negative with an imaginary positivity.

A factitious double totality is thus determined by/with limitation games between those pseudo-absolutes: nature and spirit.

Already it is not reality we are dealing with but a construct built up from *one* point of view. The nature and spirit in question are particulars that take themselves to be the absolute because of a failure to accept their limits.

It is, therefore, germane to question their status as *one(s)* and as universal(s) in terms of their particularity(ies).

Take those two parts of human kind, men and women. It is wrong for them to be brought back to *one*. What reason demonstrates by such a reduction is its impotence or immaturity: man is to be the head to the body, woman. It would seem, then, that human kind has not reached the age of reason. It is still suspended between divinity and animality. As if man were the divine for the female animal realm.

A little phenomenology could nevertheless show us that man is closer to animality than woman, unless reproduction is taken to be a sign of belonging to the animal realm, man-god being a creator only, which is to say non-human. In fact, man is engendered, not created. Yet, it is as if in wishing to be God man has lost the culture of his own body. As if he has yet to attain human status. We would seem to be a species of living beings in search of our identity, as men and women.

Therefore, we need to explore the existing nature and universal as a particularity, as particularities.

We should also ask ourselves whether we have begun to think or whether all we know of spirit is merely the operations of the understanding. In other words: we argue and debate within a field and with logical and grammatical tools defined in such a way that we cannot really think. The horizon of understanding we have debars us from that thought. We discuss, we reason, but we do not think. We finish back at square one, having produced natural and spiritual entropy along the way.

For example, the course the dialectic takes in its process of negation needs to be rethought in relation to natural immediacy, to its conception of the *in-itself* and the *for-itself*, and to its definition of the sensible dimension.

For the very same reason, all treatises on the passions or on reason need to be reconsidered and rewritten. Indeed, the sensible is not as simple or unitary as people think. Tradition usually attributes it to a single subject. Little consideration is given to the fact that the sensible is often divided, especially between two subjects. And if this dimension is discussed, it is treated in the passive-active, or agent-object mode, a method that still does not deal with the interactions between *two* free subjects. Which gives rise to this paradox in our thought: it leaves passion solitary. Is it surprising if our reason is content with a single subject? It goes round in circles in its auto-affection, all else being related, assimilated to it. Only a God can guarantee this autonomy, this confusion of the particular and the absolute. But this God also demands an indefinite estrangement from the sensible or its inversion in a reason that then remains too closely linked to the understanding. Leaving the sensible unthought endlessly taints reason with dogmatism, with madness and prevents it from realizing itself as the measure of the spirit.

Thus it is from the natural that we should start over in order to refound reason. This natural is neither simple nor universal, except, perhaps, in some of its elements: air, for instance. But air itself varies in terms of density, heat, etc., and is not, therefore, universal matter as such even though without it there can be no universal.

The natural, aside from the diversity of its incarnations or ways of appearing, is at least *two*: male and female. This division is not secondary nor unique to human kind. It cuts across all realms of the living which, without it, would not exist. Without sexual difference, there would be no life on earth. It is the manifestation of and the condition for the production and reproduction of life. Air and sexual difference may be the two dimensions vital for/to life. Not taking them into account would be a deadly business.

But let us return to nature. Restricting ourselves to human kind, let us state that neither man nor woman can manifest nor experience its totality. Each gender possesses or represents only one part of it. This reality is both very simple and quite foreign to our way of thinking.

It is evident that female and male corporeal morphology are not the same and it therefore follows that their way of experiencing the sensible and of constructing the spiritual is not the same. Moreover, women and men have different positions in relation to genealogy. For them to become the same is but an artifice. Only by submitting to authoritarian law do they become equal. But they then cease to be consonant with reality. A model of humanity is imposed that estranges man and woman from themselves. As such they do not fulfill themselves but conform to an idea of what it is to be human, of what the human being is.

This is a question that, for various reasons, we are readdressing in our time, finding scant satisfaction in the answers previously put forward.

The return to nature can be done by scientific means. If we go down this road, we either go too far or not far enough. Science has not always asked the relevant questions regarding the physiological differences between women and men. It has stuck to stating certain obvious facts: woman makes love and gives birth to children, she can breast-feed, she has several specific illnesses related to her morphology, etc. These realities are self-evident. They are not the result of intellectual hypotheses. And so one might well wonder if women are closer to the vegetable world than to the animal world, as was claimed by certain ancient philosophers, and particularly by female cultures, although, it is true, in different ways. Could it be that in this proximity there lies an accurate explanation of her relation to passivity? Woman's receptivity would not be restricted to her relation to man alone but would extend to the natural economy, especially the cosmic one, with which her equilibrium and growth are more closely associated. Her so-called passivity would not then be part of an active/passive pair of opposites but would signify a different economy, a different relation to nature and to the self that would amount to attentiveness and to *fidelity* rather than *passivity*. A matter, therefore, not of pure receptivity but of a movement of growth that never ultimately estranges itself from corporeal existence in a natural milieu. In which case, becoming is not cut off from life or its placing. It is not extrapolated from the living nor founded in a deadly character. It remains attentive to growth: physiological, spiritual, relational. In this way it masters nothing in a definitive fashion, and reason is no more than a measure, not an appropriation. As a measure, it is different for man and woman. Denying their difference(s) leads to the excess of the unmeasured.

It would be a matter of setting into motion a passive and retroactive intentionality: to become aware of being a woman or a man, and wanting to become one. It is by recognizing this that I am able to bring my intentions in line with my reality. Thus there is no longer any simple projection or natural immediacy; rather my intentions are regulated by who I am. Intention is subsequently located in a context devoid of necessary phantasies and without an imposed origin. It is moved or determined by a project but does not have to be phantasmatic, imaginary or invented. My project is regulated on the basis of my natural identity. The intention is to assure its cultivation so that I may become who I am. Equally, it is to spiritualize my nature in order to create with the other.

This creation is the transition to another stage of History. It is a liberation of the reality of sex and gender from subjection to a metaphysics or religion that leaves them to an uncultured and instinctual fate. This dimension becomes the locus and a source of energy for a culture of life without reducing the natural to procreation. The path of dialectical creation for two also offers us a way to emerge from a critique of patriarchy that might well prove nihilistic if it is not accompanied by a definition of new values founded on natural reality and having universal validity.

The universal thus results from a retroactive and non-projective constitution, from a return to reality and not from an artificial construct. I belong to the universal in recognizing that I am a woman. This woman's singularity is in having a particular genealogy and history. But belonging to a gender represents a universal that exists prior to me. I have to accomplish it in relation to my particular destiny.

The ingathering (*recueillement*) of spirit's[1] into the self has yet to occur, in that man has not moved on from a pure and simple intuition—namely, that he represents human kind. Man has not pulled himself out of his immediate being-there to consider himself as half of humanity. He has imagined that spiritual becoming can be realized on the basis of *one* and not *two*, even genealogically. In this perspective, we might indeed be going towards *one* but we do not come from *one*: we are engendered by *two* and Man as a man is born of another. From the time he is born he is thus in relation with another, with an other gender. But in patriarchal mythologies becoming on the basis of *one* has been inscribed as origin, the *two* continuing to thrive socially in female cultures.

Since he has not pulled himself out of his intuitive natural immediacy—I represent humanity—man has not begun to think. He lives in a pseudo-nature, between reality and spirituality; these have been disconnected from one another by a cultural epoch (our own) in which philosophy, as Hegel would say, is still in a state of *somnambulism* rather than a state of *awakening*. Man has not raised himself above a state of immediate unity with nature, so he dreams of being the whole. He dreams that he alone is nature and that it is up to him to undertake the spiritual task of differentiating himself from (his) nature and from himself.

This process takes time, Hegel writes. Hence, the history of philosophy has had to unfold over centuries in a sort of somnambulism in order to perceive its end or aim, its completion or its limit, its horizon. It remains for us to go beneath the origin so as to learn how to ingather ourselves within ourselves and to think. For thinking on the basis of man as *one* is still not thinking. And the labor of the negative thus put to work, into operation, is not a real negative, even if it is mortification.

From this perspective, it is strange that the philosopher, like the devout man, should have imagined for centuries that thinking or praying have to be sacrifices. It is also significant that in our cultures man thinks or prays by estranging himself from his body, and that thinking or praying do not assist him in becoming incarnate, becoming flesh. Yet, if thinking means becoming aware of one's natural immediacy, that does not mean it has to be sacrificed. Rather, sacrifice is a sign of a lack of contemplation (*recueillement*) and thought. It is but a fairly blind act (acting out, the psychoanalyst would say), speech or gesture addressed to an often absent or abstract addressee, a pre-supposition at the entrance to the world of consciousness. But this is mistaken. Take this as an example: do we have to fell a tree before cultivating it? If that were the case, what would we cultivate? An idea of the tree, but not the tree itself.

There are some similarities between our philosophy and this error.

Man is not, in fact, absolutely free. That is not to say that he is enslaved to a nature and he must overcome it. Nor does it mean he is a slave. He is *limited*. His natural completion lies in *two* humans. Man knows of only one part of human nature, yet this limit is the condition of becoming and of creation.

Man does not, therefore, have to consider his nature a burden, nor does he have to invent a second (abstract and unreal) human nature for himself, any more than he has to neutralize the difference between man and woman in the name of a factitious equality. He should rather understand that he represents only half of humanity but it is this condition that permits him to postulate the infinite without an *anti-natural* labor of the negative. The fact of being half enables the whole to be constructed without denying what is. Taking the whole as its point of departure, becoming is forced to deny the whole in order to develop. Hegel, like most people, forgets that natural immediacy is not, in a certain sense, absolute nor simple immediacy. In nature itself, nature meets its limit. This limit is indeed found in *generation*, but it is also, horizontally, in the *difference* between female and male. Besides, these two dimensions come together.

It is a mistake, therefore, to claim to be free and sovereign over nature. As I am only half of the world, I am not free in the way this is generally conceived. I am free, on the other hand, and as I should be, to be what or who I am: one half of human kind. In that sense, and in that sense only, right—my right—is a function of respect for life.

Note

1. The noun *recueillement* generally signifies contemplation or meditation (withdrawl); the verb *recueillir* means to gather in or to collect. As a philosophical term Irigaray intends *recueillement* to connote at once the return into the self, being with the self, and the notion of realization. Its meaning may be situated within a Hegelian dialectical process (albeit a non-teleological one), and it draws upon Nietzsche's return and Heidegger's *legein*, *logos* and *mitsein*. Given that the standard English translation of *recueillement* as *ingathering* in order to distinguish it from the Heideggerian term, while still conveying the sense of a process of returning movement and retaining the

more familiar connotations of gathering and withdrawl it has within the text. (Tr.)

~ 3 ~

Sexual Difference as Universal

Things could be thought differently. What we know of humanity still relates to its needs: its need to eat, to sleep, to move; its need for community or sociality, for God, for the affirmation of a human or divine power in order to exist. We know nothing of anything beyond needs. This emphasis upon needs enables the question of sexual difference to be shelved. It is quite possible to believe that woman and man have the same need to eat, to sleep, etc. These needs may appear to be universal or neutral. But we are only dealing with needs. In all probability, our culture has still not gone beyond, or has reverted to, the stage of need.

Given this situation, neither Marxism nor psychoanalysis is, in their standard formulations or applications, of much use in helping us to progress, quite the contrary.

Language itself is generally restricted to the level of needs, including the need to master nature, objects and others, especially by naming them. Linguists who turn their attention to the need for language often go no further than considering connotation or denotation. In their view, language apparently serves its purpose in denoting: "This meadow is green," "Pass me the salt," or in expressing personal feelings, "I hate this or that," "This weather is awful," "It's a beautiful night," etc. This is not language specifically adapted to communication, except for communicating information. What we have is words used to express the reality required by *needs*, including the need to unburden oneself of an excess of feelings.

Even the question of God can be treated in the same way. And it is quite wrong for us to imagine God as the highest level of spirit as long as we are incapable of speaking to ourselves. He is, He is nothing more than, the keystone of the order that still leaves us silent. He guarantees the social order that corresponds to a particular era. Yet this heaven-bound projection of a social order should—even for God himself, if I may say so—spiritually evolve, particularly when it comes to sexual difference.

And so the social organization we have had for centuries is a patriarchal one. It is a function of a civilization constructed by man, a between-men society, with woman being the property of any and everyman; natural property, domestic property.

It is a society which excludes between-woman sociality, separates women from one another and hence does not have a female culture. The only thing it does have is training for motherhood. In such a culture, it is to be expected, or at least it is understandable, that there will be no female identity models. This is a civilization without any female philosophy or linguistics, any female religion or politics. All of these disciplines have been set up in accordance with a male subject.

To now wish to shake off man's hold over History by advocating the neuter is to go back to the level of basic needs or to remain under the rule of money, a rule that is pseudo-neutral and which destroys identity. It is to deny yet again, and this time quite consciously, that women need a culture compatible with their nature and that human kind cannot develop a civilization without taking care to represent with validity the two genders it is in reality, and without assuring communication between them, not merely in the form of information transfers but in intersubjective exchanges.

Teleology, for man, amounts to keeping the source of the horizon in and for the self. It is not conversing with the other but rather suspending the interaction of the relation with the other in order to accomplish the self's own intention, even if it is divine in nature. The whole of Western philosophy is the mastery of the *direction* of will and thought by the subject, historically man. Nothing is changed by the fact that nowadays women have access to this, and it might even make things worse if philosophy's intention is not altered, if the subject is not reconstituted in a different way. Which would mean reaching another dimension, another level of consciousness, a level not of mastery but one that attempts to find spiritual harmony between passivity and activity, particularly in relations with nature and others. The domination of nature, the objective at the heart of the Western tradition, would cease to be the main aim of philosophy, even if or even when that domination is for a good cause, at least apparently. It would entail, beyond the enslavement to property, beyond the subject's submission to the object (which does not mean to objectivity), becoming capable of giving and receiving, of being active and passive, of having an intention that stays attuned to interactions, that is, of seeking a new economy of existence or being which is neither that of mastery nor that of slavery but rather of exchange with no preconstituted object—vital exchange, cultural exchange, of words, gestures, etc., an exchange thus able to *communicate* at times, to commune (but I'll leave aside for the moment this complex mode of communication in which every illusion is possible), beyond any exchange of objects. What we would be dealing with, then, is the establishment of another era of civilization, or of culture, in which the exchange of objects, and most particularly of women, would no longer form the basis for the constitution of a cultural order.[1]

Yet isn't it time for us to become communicating subjects? Have we not exhausted our other possibilities, indeed, our other desires? Isn't it time for us to become capable not only of speech but also of speaking to *one another*? Which is not the same thing at all. Hence, there is a difference in subjective economy between the hierarchical transmission of an already established discourse and language, order and law, and the exchange of a meaning between us here and now. The first model of transmission or instruction is more parental, more genealogical, more hierarchical; the second more horizontal and intersubjective. The first model risks enslavement to the past, the second opens up a present in order to construct a future. The first model operates by way of transmitted dependency, the second by way of reciprocal listening. Listening that does not exclude respect, especially for the other's experience, for the unique contribution *he* or *she* makes to culture beyond the transfer of information. The first model is not, strictly speaking, a model of communication. It is, at best, an information model, constituting knowledge as an aggregate of information and as the power it is likely to confer within institutions, in the opinion of colleagues or followers. The second model offers itself as an opening to a field of communication, as a world of the creation and exchange of thought and culture in which no man or woman can become master or slave for fear of destroying the given objective.

As for the opening up of this field, the relation between man and woman is paradigmatic; it is the groundless ground of communication, the creative and generative locus, which is natural and spiritual, passive and active at the same time.

Such a relation can only come about if man renounces the domination of nature and of the economy of subjectivity, and if woman has the ability to govern her nature so that she becomes subjectivity. Which means women must construct an objective identity model enabling them to situate themselves as women and not merely as mothers or as equals in their relations with man, with men.

There are thus two acts to be carried out almost simultaneously: an act of constitution and an act of interpretation and departure from a cultural identity, departure from a land of exile that falsely separates man and woman, where man is attributed mechanistic and technological norms and powers, and woman physiological and affective ones. Male becoming, depending more upon the understanding, may appear to be more rational, but it is not insofar as it follows a natural immediacy that remains unthought and unorganized: the fact of belonging to a male sex or gender. The second identity model, the one imposed upon women, may appear to be more individualistic and capricious, but it follows a rationality which the present society cannot do without. Valorized by society as a mother, nurturer and housewife (the community needs children to make up the future work-force, as defenders of the nation and as reproducers of society, aside from the fact that the family unit is the most profitable one for the State in that much of the work that is done within it goes unpaid, for example), woman is deprived of the possibility of interiorizing her female identity. It is imposed upon her as pure exteriority. And that's one of the reasons why she herself, just like the society that defines her, privileges the mother-son relationship; the mother-daughter relationship reminds woman, women, of their lack of subjective identity, and arouses affects for which there is no corresponding cultural organization. This relationship is thus one of the areas where it is important to work for the establishment of mediations, of relations between the in-itself and the for-itself for woman. We must, in short, define a culture of the female.

The sphere of mother-daughter and daughter-mother relationships obviously invalidates all those straightforward claims to equality between the sexes. Women have a different individual, and to some extent collective, history from men. We need to interpret and construct that history spiritually in order to open up another era in our culture, an era in which the subject is no longer *one*, solipsistic, egocentric and potentially imperialistic, but which rather respects differences, and particularly the difference inscribed in nature and subjectivity themselves: sexual difference.

Without doubt, the most appropriate content for the universal is sexual difference. Indeed, this content is both real and universal. Sexual difference is an immediate natural given and it is a real and irreducible component of the universal. The whole of human kind is composed of women and men and of nothing else. The problem of race is, in fact, a secondary problem—except from a geographical point of view?—which means we cannot see the wood for the trees, and the same goes for other cultural diversities—religious, economic and political ones.

Sexual difference probably represents the most universal question we can address. Our era is faced with the task of dealing with this issue, because, across the whole world, there are, there are only, men and women.

The culture of this universal is yet to be. The individual has been considered as a particular without an adequate interpretation of this universal that is in her or him: woman or man.

In the history of our culture, there's much talk of *I*. *Thou* (*Tu*) and *the other* are also evoked—whether with reference to my neighbor or to a totally other God, the *Thou* of certain philosophers or a theology that forgets that this you (*tu*) is generally a *he*. But these *I*'s and *you*'s, which seem self-evident within the bounds of a delimited field, remain vague and abstract. We only have to talk about the concrete existence of living men and women for us to falter over the question of who is this *I* and who is this *you*. *Do you love me?* the woman says to the man. *I wonder if I am loved*, he replies. How can *we* be formed, then?

Women and men will have to be granted a real identity, a natural and spiritual one, and not hobble along, one foot in pure nature (repro-duction), the other in an abstract culture, if *we* is to be formed. The need is more pressing and imperative for women but it does exist for men, too.

Being *we* means being at least *two*, autonomous, different. This *we* still has no place, neither between the human genders or sexes, nor in the public realm where male citizens (women not yet being full citizens) form a social whole in the form of *one* plus *one* plus *one*, a sort of undifferentiated magma under the monarchical or oligarchic authority (even in supposedly democratic systems) of a male kind of power. Here individualism is both postulated as the norm and turns out to be an impossibility inasmuch as the autonomy of citizens remains to be constructed, as does, paradigmatically, that of the men and women of which the public realm is constituted.

We have yet to construct this cultural and political program. It requires all leaders, whether human or divine, to descend from their thrones in order to be first of all simply a man, or a woman.

Note

1. I am referring to the work of Lévi-Strauss, for example.

~ 4 ~

Donning a Civil Identity

At the present time, society is controlled by money. And slavery lies, above all, in that fact. All human beings, or almost all, are dependent upon money. The only exceptions to this are some peasants or vegetarian hermits, a few rare groups living on wild berries and sheltering themselves with natural materials.

Levels of dependence vary; some men and women have more money than others, some women and men are more autonomous than others. But the system of production in which we live means that all of us, men and women, are dependent upon money and dependent upon one another.

This creates a society without any freedom, with sudden aggressive outbursts from individuals, groups, or nations. Everyone wants to assert that their subjectivity, their resources, their culture, or their power permits them to make a special case for themselves amidst the general state of dependence and interdependence. For a while, they become the focus of attention; sub-systems are organized in a different way but fundamentally things remain the same. Take the Gulf crisis, which restricted some forms of production and gave rise to others. And the whole situation merely reinforces interdependency and dependence upon money.

How can we get away from this generalized and growing alienation of the person? Money has to be removed from its position of dominance in civil society, which entails going back to the reality—including the natural reality—of persons, in order to reconstruct the law—and rights.

Two natural necessities dominate societies. One of them may appear to be neuter, unmarked by the sexual: we all have to breathe, feed, clothe and house ourselves. Our societies are controlled by this need, which, rightful as it is, accords money a power that is totally disproportionate— a power rarely questioned by democratic regimes even though it inevitably leads to new hierarchies between rich and poor and between affluent and impoverished countries, along with a redistribution system based upon pity and upon appeals to share, which potentially exacerbate loss of human dignity and authoritarian relations between people.

Of course, sharing is better than leaving someone to die of starvation. But this always involves the power of some over others, a power mediated by money.

In addition to need, there is another dimension in the person, that of desire, which is linked to energy, particularly sexual energy. This dimension of the person as sexed is important for social production and reproduction: without it, there is no society. Yet the dignity and necessity of sexual difference goes unrecognized. Civil society remains a slave to money and to its domination. Money has become the universal mediator. But, in money, humanity has alienated its freedom and its culture.

The fact remains that we are men and women. And that this constitutes a living universal. It is a universal related to our real person, to his or her needs, abilities and desires. The particularity of this universal is that it is divided into two. Thus, respecting the difference between woman and man is itself culture. It goes beyond natural immediacy. If man and woman respect each other as those two halves of the universe that they represent, then by recognizing the other they overcome their immediate instincts and drives. They are spiritual humans from the fact of recognizing that they do not represent the whole of the person and that the other cannot belong to them as their own property. In sexual difference, the negative as limit is present from the very fact of respecting natural reality as constitutive of the subject.

Sexual difference is, as it were, the most powerful motor of a dialectic without masters or slaves. This dialectic does not have to be tragic because it renders obsolete a certain number of oppositions required for the dialectic of a unique and solipsistic subject. It necessitates a law of persons appropriate to their natural reality, that is, to their sexed identity.[1]

By virtue of this law: Universal and particular are reconciled, but they are two. Each man and each woman is a particular individual, but universal through their gender, to which must correspond an appropriate law, a law common to all men and to all women.

In the face of the universal that law represents, each person or individual is thus passive and active: she or he receives the right to be woman or man, as he or she is born man or woman. In this capacity, they enter into and are protected by society and they must respect, cultivate, and historically develop this right.

No longer does the natural, then, have to be abolished in the spiritual rather the concrete spiritual consists in the cultivation of the natural. An appropriate civil law is required as mediator for this cul-tivation. That law concerns the needs and desires of real persons considered as such: for life and its respective qualities, for instance. It cannot be reduced to questions of property, which is the case for most current civil law.

In this respect, making law compatible with real persons will enable us to overcome the splits and contradictions between subjectivity and objectivity concerning needs and demands that arise from a person's own will. As for objectivity, it gives laws a content that is not only external or formal but necessitated by the very nature of the person.

In this way, to recognize an identity in oneself is itself to overcome instinctual and egological immediacy by recognizing the negative in the self. "I am sexed" implies, "I am not everything." Identifying with my gender amounts to entering the world of mediation provided I recognize the existence of the other gender. There will thus no longer be the simple identity of my will with itself since respecting my nature as generic identity constrains the immediacy of my will. But this constraint does not emanate from an abstract or impersonal law. It is established on the basis of the objectivity of who I actually am. Before being limited by others, I am limited by myself owing to the objectivity of my sexed body and to the particularity that ensues from my inscription in a genealogy. In this sense, there is no immediate subjectivity. This is an incorrect concept, notion or expression. It is just as incorrect to say that my will could be identical, equal or similar to that of everyone else. It must be distinguishable in order to be appropriate to myself and positive in relation to others while respecting their own identity. The principle of morality and ethics thus consists concretely in the respect for real differences, of which sexual difference is at one and the same time the most particular and the most universal model, a model in relation to which genealogy is a secondary, though necessary, paradigm.

Respecting the law thus becomes, with this definition, a moral and ethical task. It regulates the spiritual behavior of every individual—man or woman—and regulates the organization of society. In this way, religion ceases to serve as a subjective buttress for or against respect for the other *qua* other and social power is taken away from authoritarian control and management by masters. It falls to each woman and man to exercise the rights and duties of citizenship. Should there be elected representatives, their task is to make sure that civil law is respected.

Law can thus function as a dialectical tool between subjective will in the self and for the self. Law constitutes an objectivity. Yet, if it accords with the reality of the person, it has a subjective aspect. It guarantees a subjectivity faithful to itself, one not defined by the object and not alienated in it.

The law of persons represents the guardian of subjectivity, enabling it to develop without alienating itself in possession. The law of persons leaves open the possibility of subjectivity's developing without alienation in possession—which anchors it in the past. The law of persons regulates relations between people in which questions of having, of competition for possession, are not an issue; these all too often define the subjectivity of citizens, and as such reduce them to petty masters forever fighting among themselves.

Property primarily corresponds (in this sense) to being itself, to the right and duty of each man and woman to be and to become what he or she is. Citizenship is thus no longer characterized by the accumulation of possessions protected by a civil law. It is a function of being born, actually and not abstractly. Citizens are those women and men who are listed in the registers of the civil state. Law is thus no longer a straightforward obligation emanating from an omnipotent master, who is both legislator and executor. Law guarantees the identity of each man and woman and his or her own mastery of that identity. The status of citizen is consequently unrelated to the quantity and hierarchy of possessions, whether property or capital, or symbolic possessions. This right is due each woman and man by birth. Everyone has the right and duty to be what he or she is.

Such a right is the condition of a true democracy. Each man and woman is, from birth, a full citizen.

In the face of this law, hierarchical power pales into insignificance, even genealogical power. Thus, a girl or boy enjoys the right to be a citizen from birth. As such, each woman and man is protected by the State, against their family if need be. The family is thus no longer the locus of an all-powerful authority. Civil society tempers this power. And in the same way, natural law is no longer merely familial since civil identity is related to a natural identity: of woman or man.

To turn law into legislation concerning primarily persons and not property means turning it over to its principal and motivating role or function for each man and woman. The choice of investing in any particular thing, or in any particular property, is secondary compared to the right to exist.

In this perspective, law for the most part ceases to be defined from the standpoint of the accumulation and ownership of property, thus from a position of relative exteriority in relation to persons.

Law is protection for life and the means to cultivate interiority. It attests to the fact that differences in the properties and qualities of life—being woman or man, for example—require a civil law that is guaranteed by the State. Being inscribed into the registers of civil society is to

~

draw up a contract between the State and a newborn male or female citizen. Consequently, law concerns not merely contingent matters but the very existence of the citizens who make up the State.

The limitations of customary legal procedures, the opposition between formal law and individual subjective will, should be clarified in this form of jurisdiction. And so should the limitations of all actions emanating from a subjectivity with no objective legal framework: vengeance, abuse of parental power, violence against women and children, the use of religion against respect and freedom for the person, etc.

What type of language could be offered a person, a group, or a crowd to make them free, give them life and unify them while respecting reason? What else could be offered other than a civil law that makes it a priority to provide a right to exist and makes respect for the other obligatory? Isn't it excessive to call for respect for the nation in view of the almost complete absence of individual right as far as persons are concerned? Nations nowadays are male peoples anyway. In order to redefine a law that is just we necessarily have to redefine individual right relating to real persons, women and men of all ages. In the light of such a right civil authority will become a service and not a power. No longer will it dictate the law, legislation; it will ensure that the rights of each man and woman are put into practice.

In the terms of such a right, the law makes the protection of life a priority. Life is above all always individual, personal. It is also always sexed. In protecting these dimensions of the reality of the people who constitute it, society opens up conduits for attraction and distancing between all men and women instead of subjecting individuals to a generally abstract juridical machinery. These conduits are principally determined by their belonging to a sex but they are always tempered and regulated by civil legislation. Social relations are thus organized according to sentiments which are in varying degrees physical, affective or spiritual, a truth that is in varying degrees empirical or speculative, and a culture and politics founded on the basis of reality and life. A structure, or structures, of identification and of spiritualization which establish relations and communication between living persons replace structures that put into place more or less deadly mechanisms of power. Processes of cultural integration and interiorization take over from external structures of crowd domination. Such structures have been constituted for centuries, and are ever more so, in accordance with sexual models described by Freud as those belonging to masculine sexuality, the only one capable of libido in his view. Hence, they comprise accumulations and overloads which periodically demand a discharge and a return to homeostasis. If social models were organized in accordance with the reality of living persons, they would entail the constant regulation and constant sharing of energy without the tension and hardening only resolved by cathartic catastrophes. It may be possible for a harmony and growth respectful of life to exist through a constant balancing between attraction and retention. And this would maintain and retain an energy of return for each man and woman, an energy that serves life and culture, prevents ill-considered and short-lived forms of growth, and protects and retains what has been gained, particularly with respect to life and civilization.

In our abstract and commercial cultures, it is actually only in sexuality that the return to self takes place (God generally being defined as an outside-the-self), but this return amounts to an annulment, a return to zero for energy and the interiorization of desire. The child alone is supposed to remain the outcome of the labor of love, which puts love in the service of genealogy and justifies a thinker like Hegel defining the child as the death of its parents. Unfortunately, this death does not bring culture to the child nor to the lovers: the man and woman. The child is a product of their corporal relationship, which does not rule out spiritual will in engendering. But the child maintains the outside-the-self of the lovers' desire. The interiority of the love between the woman and the man is denied if this love is subordinate to the obligation to have a child and is only recognized as being parental and reproductive love.

The end of an era of History: this is in a certain sense what Hegel did not imagine. He considered his own time and system as capable of realizing the end of History. But his theory, without doubt the most powerful of the Western philosophies, can itself be subject to a dialectic. And so, in Hegel's conception of History, it is possible to analyze a for-itself appropriate to the male subject alone, a for-itself which Hegel did not interpret in this way. The spirit Hegel speaks of turns out to be less absolute than he thought. It can be subject to a dialectic in its for-itself and its in-itself. Indeed, if the for-itself remains unanalyzed in its singularity, spirit contains a non-spiritualized substance and subjective.

Today various symptoms of this are evident:

— the decline of History's spirituality
— the subjective and objective injustice prevalent in various domains: law, religion, culture
— the inability of subjectivity to master the current era, when it comes to technology, for example, but also in the transmission of information.

Technology in fact constitutes an in-itself that man can no longer entirely dialecticize into a for-itself. The reign of absolute spirit has become an impossibility. Although man may have thought he could master nature, he cannot, at present, accomplish the mastery of technology.

The dialectic must therefore be reapplied to the unfolding of History itself so as to determine an era and enable it to be situated in the development of spirit. It must be rethought as a method in relation to historical discoveries and necessities, a method useful for assuring the constitution and the temporality of male and female subjectivities, as well as those of the couples and communities that these real subjects form.

And so the function of the negative would be different. It would become the recognition of the limits, natural ones included, of the self and its spirit. The negative is thus no longer in the power of man alone, and he is no longer the only deciding factor. On the other hand, *I*, human subject, can decide whether or not to consent to this, whether to let the other, and in part the world, be and become, or whether to set myself in opposition to their existence and growth. I can agree to recognize a reality that is foreign to me, that will never be mine, but which determines me and with which I am in relation. I can attempt to communicate and dialogue with the real other, before constituting *you* as total-other, a *Thou* that may well be just another me, support for the perpetuation of the same, the eternal guardian of my image, my ideal.

Such a change in the nature of the constitution of subjectivity and the recognition of the other as another, irreducible to me and unthinkable in terms of my spirit, could be the opening-up of a period of History yet to come. For to exist, we need transformations in the law and in the symbolic processes of language and the languages of discourse. That is why I have decided to pay particular attention to these domains in this sketch for a possible felicity within History.

Note

1. On this subject, see: *Sexes et Parentés*, Editions de Minuit, 1987, trans. *Sexes and Genealogies*, Gillian C. Gill (Columbia University Press, 1993): "Introduction" and "The Universal as Mediation"; *Le temps de la différence*, translation forthcoming, Karen Montin, Athlone Press and *Je, tu, nous*, op. cit.

~ 5 ~

The Other: Woman

Issues to do with women's liberation generate a good deal of misunderstanding, confusion and pointless conflict. I would like to try to interpret a few of these associated with my own work. To do this, I will take three interrelated examples: 1) the meaning of the title and subtitle of *Speculum*, 2) the view or belief that I changed theoretical and political direction with *An Ethics of Sexual Difference* 3) accusations that I have been untrue or a traitor to the women's cause owing to my work with certain mixed-sex political groups, the Italian Communist Party among them.

In the title of *Speculum*, as throughout the whole book, I played on words, on meanings, to enable a different truth to appear. Thus, *speculum* denotes a gynecological instrument, though at an earlier period in our culture this term was used to denote the most faithful expression of reality possible. *Speculum mundi*, for example, was not an uncommon title and was what I had in mind. It signifies mirror of the world—not so much the reflection of the world in a mirror as the thought of the reality or objectivity of the world through a discourse. Unfortunately, this second meaning, the most important in terms of what I intended, is less well-known. My primary intention is, therefore, generally poorly understood, which is especially obvious in the interpretations and translations given to the subtitle: *De l'autre femme*.

Naturally, I took risks in writing the title and sub-title in the way I did in French. It might have been less ambiguous if I had written it like this: *Speculum, De l'autre: femme*. Then the title of this first book dealing with female identity could have been, in Italian, for example: *Speculum, A proposito de l'altro in quanto donna*, or, *Speculum, De l'altro: donna*. The actual translation: *L'altra donna* does not correspond to the meaning of my thought and the English translation: *Speculum, Of the other woman*, is clearly even further from what I intended; *Speculum, On the other woman* would have been a more suitable choice, or better still, *On the other: woman*. The same goes for the Spanish translation of the title. The German translators opted for *Speculum, Spiegel des andere Geschlecht*. This option might seem preferable since it avoids the possible insistence upon a relation between two women but there is still too much emphasis on the mirror and it leaves out the allusion to a dialectical relation between a woman and herself as other.

My intention in choosing the title and subtitle of *Speculum, De l'autre femme*, related to the project of constituting the world—and not only the specular world—of the other as a woman. There was no question, then, of my holding up some mirror so that it reflects an other or the other woman. In *Speculum*, the question of the mirror figures as interpretation and criticism of the enclosure of the Western subject in the *Same*, even in those propositions concerning the need to use a different mirror for the constitution of female identity.

The meaning of the title and subtitle: *Speculum, De l'autre femme*, does not, therefore, refer to a purely empirical relation between (two?) women, nor to an already constituted relation of Luce Irigaray with *L'autre femme* (l'altra donna, the other woman, and so on). Who would this other woman be given that no female generic yet exists as representation or as content of an ideality for woman?

The other—*De l'autre femme*—should be taken as a substantive. In French, the other is supposed to denote man and woman, just as it is in other languages, such as Italian and English. In the subtitle of *Speculum*, I wanted to indicate that the other is not in fact neuter, either grammatically or semantically, and that it is not, or is no longer, possible to use the same words indiscriminately for the masculine and the feminine. Now this practice is widespread in philosophy, religion, and politics. There is talk of the other's existence, love of the other, concern for the other, etc., without it being asked whom or what this other represents. This lack of definition of the alterity of the other has left all thought, the dialectical method included, in a state of paralysis, in an idealistic dream appropriate to a single subject (the male), in the illusion of a unique absolute, and has left religion and politics to an empiricism profoundly lacking in ethics when it comes to respect between persons. For if the other is not defined in his or her actual reality, there is only an other me, not real others: the other may then be *more* or *less* than I am, might have *more* or *less* than me. And so it may represent (my) absolute perfection or greatness, the Other: God, Master, *logos*; it might denote the most insignificant or the most destitute: children, the ill, the poor, the outsider; it might name the one I consider to be my equal. It is not the other we are really dealing with but the same: inferior, superior, or equal to me.

However, before wishing to make the other one's equal, I think it is fair to ask: who am I who asks the other to be my equal? And then: in accordance with which measure, which order, which power, which Other (?) will these so-called equals be brought together and organized socially?

Between man and woman, there really is otherness: biological, morphological, relational. To be able to have a child constitutes a difference, but also being born a girl or a boy of a woman, who is of the same or the other gender as oneself, as well as to be or to appear corporeally with differing properties and qualities. Some of our prosperous or naive contemporaries, women and men, would like to wipe out this difference by resorting to monosexuality, to the unisex and to what is called identification: even if I am bodily a man or woman, I can identify with, and so be, the other sex. This new opium of the people annihilates the other in the illusion of a reduction to identity, equality and sameness, especially between man and woman, the ultimate anchorage of real alterity. The dream of dissolving material, corporeal or social identity leads to a whole set of delusions, to endless and unresolvable conflicts, to a war of images or reflections and to powers being accredited to somebody or other more for imaginary or narcissistic reasons than for their actual abilities. Unless money itself is becoming the sole stake in ideality.

Man and woman should not be abandoned to a mode of functioning in which woman is hierarchically inferior to man—to positively construct alterity between them is a task for our time. The aim of *Speculum* is to construct an objectivity that facilitates a dialectic proper to the female subject, meaning specific relations between her nature and her culture, her same and her other, her singularity and the community, her interiority and her exteriority, etc. *Speculum* and my other works insist upon the irreducibility—either subjective or objective—of the sexes to one another, which requires us to establish a dialectic of the relation of woman to herself and of man to himself, a double dialectic therefore, enabling a real, cultured and ethical relation between them.[1] It is both a philosophical and a political task. It should not be confused with auto-biographical narrative, with theoretical propositions that ignore the labor of the negative vis-à-vis elementary subjectivity, with immediate affect, with self-certainty, mimetic or recapitulative intuitive truth, with historical narrative, etc.

Having commented at some length on the title of *Speculum*, I believe I have explained why *An Ethics of Sexual Difference* followed on from *Speculum*, as well as why it was quite logical for me to want to work with the Italian Communist Party, in that they recognize the importance of the other, as a woman, (*l'altro in quanto donna*) for the operation of a just dialectic in History. Moreover, History cannot do without the existence of two human subjects, man and woman, if it is to get away from master-slave relationships.

Making the difference between the sexes the motor of the dialectic's becoming also means being able to renounce death as sovereign master so that we may at last give our care to the expansion of life: natural and spiritual, individual and collective, life.

But many women, and men for that matter, still do not believe that woman can be anything other than the complement to man, his inverse, his scraps, his need, his other. Which means that she cannot be truly other. The other that she is remains trapped in the economy or the horizon of a single subject. In *Speculum*, I wanted to question this female alterity defined from a male subject's point of view. I questioned myself as identified in this way: the other of/for man and man alone.

Asked about my method for initiating the thinking of sexual difference, I could say that I have several or that I try to find the most suitable one, but there is one method that I used to write *Speculum* and continue to use regularly—inversion. It is a method used by more recent philosophers: Marx inverts Hegel, Nietzsche inverts Platonism, and the problematics of the return—present in other philosophies, such as Heidegger's—are in some respect problematics of inversion. There is a notable difference, though, in that Marx inverts Hegel, Nietzsche inverts Platonism, the problematics of the return invert History, and so on. Thus it is a case of inverting something exterior to oneself and already constituted as such. In Freudian terms, we might say that it approximates to the murder of the father, the overthrow of the ancestor or his *oeuvre* by a son wishing to become an adult.

In my case, it was more a question of inverting myself. I was the other of/for man, I attempted to define the objective alterity of myself for myself as belonging to the female gender. I carried out an inversion of the femininity imposed upon me in order to try to define the female corresponding to my gender: the in-and-for-itself of my female nature. This process is extremely difficult to carry out and explains most of the misunderstandings about my work and thought. Unlike most women, (see Simone de Beauvoir's introduction to *The Second Sex*), I did not want to speak of the other: woman as the other-woman of/for man, of the other-woman in the male and patriarchal horizon of our culture. Nor did I want, as some have thought or written, to enact the parricide of one of my supposed masters. Not at all. I wanted to begin to define what a woman is, thus myself as a woman—and not only *a* woman but as freely belonging to the female gender or generic—by carrying out a partial process of limitation or negation relative to my natural immediacy, and relative to the representation I had been given of what I was as a woman, that is, the other of/for man, the other of male culture. Hence, I attempted to sketch out a spirituality in the feminine, and in doing so, of course, I curbed my own needs and desires, my natural immediacy, especially by thinking myself as half and only half the world, but also by calling into question the spirituality imposed on me in the culture appropriate to the male or to patriarchy, a culture in which I was the other of the Same.

Most of the works by women today aim to describe what a woman is within the horizon of a male subject's culture. In which case, some women, some of the one + one + one... (*une* + *une* + *une...*) women describe or tell their life stories. This is indeed speaking out. But then there is a plurality that seems to elude the definition of a unity: *woman*, except perhaps insofar as it is determined by man or as possible natural immediacy. More often than not, these women, or rather this female identity, still apparently originates in man. As our tradition dictates, man originates from God, and woman from man. As long as the female generic—woman—is not determined as such, this will be true. Women will remain men's or Man's creatures. With respect to themselves, and among themselves, they are unable to create, create (for) themselves, especially an ideal, for want of an identity and of mediations. They will be able to criticize their condition, complain, reject themselves or one another, but not establish a new era of History or of culture.

But some of the strongest resistance, indeed the greatest resistance, to the construction of new relations between women, and between women and men, arises wherever a new model of female identity is to be elaborated. This resistance is upheld by men in the name of their culture: they must not lose their monopoly of the model of human kind, the privilege of representing the ideal for human kind. Thus they are Man, he, He, the human generic, and women are the one + one + one (*un[e]* + *un[e]* + *un[e]*) of this human kind, which is, in fact, male. The resistance is also perpetuated by women who are not used to defining themselves in human terms as women and have difficulty in acknowledging a female model of identity. They are often the most virulent in calling for equality with men and for the neutralization of female identity and the female ideal. Thus, women have a strange idea of democracy. As they have no rights proper to them, democracy is often, in their view, the reduction of women to the lowest common denominator. Rarely do they recognize in a woman's value a possible model of identity, whether this be the person herself or in her theory or thought. Unfortunately, women are the first to say that woman does not exist and cannot do so. Which means they refuse to accept a generic identity for the female. This denial eliminates the possibility of constituting a culture of two sexes, two genders. We remain in the horizon in which man is the model of human kind, and within this human kind, there are empirical women or there are natural entities without an identity of their own.

Women's liberation, and indeed the liberation of humanity, depends upon the definition of a female generic, that is, a definition of what woman is, not just this or that woman. For women to get away from a model of hierarchical submission to male identity we need to define the female gender, the generic identity of women.

To be able to attain this generic identity, we need to attribute value to the pronouns *he* and *she* and to their plural forms[2] as an expression of gender and we need to accord positive value to the pronoun *she* as that which designates the female gender.

It's fairly easy to state that the *I* and the *you* are not used in the same way depending upon whether the speaking subjects are women or men. Men tend to speak out more than women. In addition, men say *I* more, designate themselves as subjects of the discourse, action or condition that is being expressed more frequently than women do. Analysis of their respective statements reveals that men use *I*, women *you/the other*, but these *I* and *you* are situated within one single problematic where there are not two subjects but rather the workings of the incomplete economy of a single subject.

That said, subjectivity cannot be reduced to saying *I*; it is also signified by means of the objective generic representation of the speaking subject: *he* and *she*. Yet in the history of culture —in philosophy, theology, even linguistics—much is said about *I* and *you* and very little about *he* or *she*. With the result that we are no longer sure who *I* and *you* are in a concrete situation, since *I* and *you* are always sexed and the loss of this dimension obscures the identity of who is speaking and of the person to whom the message is addressed. Consequently, we do not have an *I* and *you* that are clearly determined and stand for a meaning, nor do we have the possibility of *we*.

To come to this *we*, consideration has to be given to how *he* and *she* operate in exchanges. *He* and *she* are figures forgotten in the history of philosophy, censured by theology, and poorly defined in linguistics, where these real partners hobble along, one foot in culture, the other in nature. While men and women do not speak out equally, if man says *I* more and woman *you* more, the gap is even greater between the use of *he* and *she* in the discourse of women and men.

Of course, in this case usage is directly induced by cultural models and codes, especially linguistic ones, which have not been thought through in terms of sexual difference: a) the human generic is designated by *he* and *he* alone; b) the mixed plural is expressed by the masculine plural, which means that in a mixed group, even with just two people, a woman has to endorse the *il(s)*,[3] especially in love; of lovers, one has to say: *ils s'aiment* (they love each other), *ils sont beaux* (they are beautiful), *ils ont fait un grand voyage* (they took a long trip), and so on. The same goes for generation: *ils ont fait un bel enfant* (they have had a lovely baby), *ils ont décidé d'avoir un enfant cette année* (they have decided to have a child this year), and so on; the woman's relationship to herself, women's relationships among themselves, and especially the relationship between mother and daughter, are thus wiped out in all mixed-sex situations; c) the masculine gender is valorized at the expense of the feminine, which means not only that *he* always takes precedence over *she* but also that masculine gender words, things belonging to the masculine gender, are valued more highly than those designating the feminine: *la secrétaire du patron* (the boss's secretary), for example, compared with *le secrétaire de l'Etat* (the Secretary of State).[4]

How can this be explained on a speculative level?

Language and its values reflect the social order and vice versa.

Language functions as a sort of inversion of the situation of the engendering of *he* in *she*. Language presents itself as a technique of appropriating *she/they (elles)* in *he/they (ils)* or an inverted hierarchy vis-à-vis the power of maternal gestation. Father-*logos* claims to be the overall engenderer compared to mother-nature. But, in this gesture—which is similar to the *fort-da* of little Hans with his bobbin[5]—man has not really thought out his relation to engendering, to the fact of being engendered: he denies it by affirming the all-powerful status of language, of his language, which cancels out the difference between the sexes, the genders and is conveyed by setting up a transcendence corresponding to a monosexual code, a Law-making-God-the-Father, etc. Which can equate to an absolute transcendence only insofar as it is appropriated to male identity, and entails reductions with respect to the constitution of female identity.

Just as the masculine's transcendence is problematic in terms of what it annuls of the reality of engendering, the establishment of this culture, which is called patriarchal, denies transcendence in the feminine. Everything that is of the feminine gender is thus less valued in this logic because it lacks any possible dimension of transcendence. Christianity's cult of mother and son is not a sign of respect for feminine transcendence, unless it is given a different interpretation.

It is this that makes a spiritual relationship between the sexes an impossibility.

Now *he* and *she* designate the objectivity of two sexed subjects. Not to give them an equally valid linguistic status is to:

— To say that as subject *I* and *you*, they do not have the same value.

— To deprive the two pronouns, the two genders, of their meanings since one term is defined by the other.

— To rule out a dialectic of the sexed subject; thus the female subject who can say *I* but without *she* remains in a subjectivism without a subjectivity-objectivity dialectic. Furthermore, an *I-you* relation between the sexes needs to go through a subjectivity-objectivity dialectic for each sex.

We need to go through this valorizing of the two pronouns *he* and *she* in order to uphold the intentionality of the *I* that operates in the relation between *I* and *you*; otherwise it becomes pathological.

In order to constitute a free and active temporality, the I-woman needs a *she* that is valorized as a pole of intentionality between *she* and *she*, *I-she* and *she-herself*.

Notes

1. See *Speculum, De l'autre femme*, pp. 266–281, *Speculum of the Other Woman*, pp. 214–226.

2. Irigaray writes the pronouns thus: *il(s)* and *elle(s)*, hence referring to both the singular and plural third person pronouns. Orally and aurally they cannot be differentiated. *Il* is the masculine/neuter pronoun, *he*, *elle* the feminine *she*; in French the plural retains its gender mark unlike the neuter *they*. However, *ils* is used for both an exclusively masculine plural and for a plural constituted by masculine and feminine substantives; *elles* is only possible as an exclusively feminine plural. The philosophical and linguistic implications of this are taken up throughout this book and in her other works. (Tr.)

3. See note 2. (Tr.)

4. With reference to this, see *Je, tu, nous*, op. cit.

5. See *"La croyance même"* and *"Le geste en psychanalyse"* in *Sexes et parentés*, trans. "Belief Itself" and "Gesture in Psychoanalysis," in *Sexes and Genealogies*, op. cit.

~ 6 ~

She Forgotten Between Use and Exchange

In French, the pronouns *il(s)* and *elle(s)* are used in a very unequal way and are not accorded equivalent value.[1] This question is one we began to examine in *Sexes et genres à travers les langues*.

There follow some new examples of these different uses drawn from the results of linguistic research which presented participants with cues different from those given during the research dealt with in that book. The main population samples questioned are those indicated on p. 80.

THE PRIVILEGE ACCORDED TO THE SUBJECT: *il(s)*

The preferential use of *il(s)* over *elle(s)* is revealed by the pronoun participants choose to use as the subject when asked to respond to cues of the type: "Make a sentence with the following word." In most cases, the cue was given orally and the response written.

1) The word: *chien* (dog)[2]

In the responses given, the percentage of those who chose *il* and those who chose *elle* is as follows (the percentage using *ils* and *elles* was negligible):

— women's responses:
  75% use *il*
  15% use *elle*

— men's responses:
  85% use *il*
  14% use *elle*

Thus, even women use *il* rather than *elle* in the subject position.

The type of sentence also differs according to whether its subject is *il* or *elle* and whether they are produced by men or women. Those utterances using *il* as subject are more stereotypical, those using *elle* as subject more context-dependent and more expressive of quality and modality. For example: *Il promène son chien* (He takes his dog for a walk), but: *Elle promène son chien tous les jours* (She takes her dog for a walk every day).

It should be noted that, if the person doing the research does not indicate that the word "*chien*" should be in the complement position in the sentence, then this word is often employed as the subject at the expense of an *elle* appearing in the response.

2) The word: *enfant* (child)[3]

In responses given by women, there are again many *il* subjects, although the percentage of *elle* subjects is higher than for the former cue.

Verbs used vary according to whether the subject is *il* or *elle*: *il s'amuse avec* (he plays with), *il aime* (he loves), while *elle nourrit* (she feeds), *elle élève* (she raises), *elle berce* (she cradles), *elle aime* (she loves), (but to a far lesser extent).

With the responses given by men, we find that in the subject position:

  79.5% use *il*
  28.5% use *elle*

and the predicates are less neutral than in the women's responses: *elle a perdu* (she has lost), *elle renie*, (she denies), *elle a expulsé son enfant* (she rejected her child), or else *elle lui donne le biberon* (she gives him/her a bottle), while *il adore* (he adores), *il aime* (he loves), *il est prévoyant vis-à-vis de son enfant* (he is caring with his child).

AVOIDANCE OF THE SUBJECT: *elle(s)*

With cues implying the use of *elle*, and even *elle se* (she herself) as the subject of the sentence—for example, this instruction: "Make a sentence with the words: *robe-se-voir*"[4]—responses reveal:

a) The avoidance of *elle* as an active subject by both sexes.

   — *Elle* very often becomes a passive object, even when apparently in the subject position: *Elle se voit/elle est visible* (she can be seen/is visible [especially by a male subject producing the statement] rather than: *Elle se voit elle-même en robe* (She sees herself in a dress).

   — The object *robe* becomes the subject: *La/cette robe se voit bien* (The/this dress stands out).

b) Avoidance of *elle se* (she herself).

   — *Elle se voit elle-même en robe* (She sees herself in a dress) is a very unusual response, especially from women, except as an allusion to day-dreams, as a conditional, etc.

   — The emphasis is on the visibility of the dress, and especially its characteristics, rather than upon the woman looking at herself. It is women particularly who do this.

There is no avoidance of *il se* (he himself) even with cues such as *robe-se-voir*, to which the response is sometimes: *Il se voit déjà en robe d'avocat* (He can already see himself in a lawyer's gown), *Il ne se voit pas en robe* (He cannot see himself wearing a dress), etc.

c) Avoidance of *elles se* (they [fem.] themselves)

   Out of 500 responses, only a very few sentences used *elles se*: *Elles se voient dans leur nouvelle robe* (They see themselves in their new dress), for example. And this choice was implicit in the cues presented, such as *elle* or *elle se*.

~

CONFIRMATION OF THE PRIVILEGE ACCORDED TO *il(s)*, *il(s) se*
AND OF THE AVOIDANCE OF *elle(s)*, *elle(s) se*

The following are examples of the sorts of responses given for several
different cues, some of which are considered further in the next chapter
or were discussed in *Sexes et genres à travers les langues*:

Pantalon-se-voir (Pants-Self-See)

Il se voit (lui) dans le pantalon de son père.
(He can see himself in his father's pants).
Le pantalon (de elle) se voit de loin.
(Her pants stand out a lot.)

Chapeau-se-voir (Hat-Self-See)

Il se trouve beau avec un chapeau.
(He thinks he looks good in a hat.)
Son chapeau (à elle) se voit.
(Her hat stands out.)

Se (Self)[5]

There is considerable use of *il se*, even in the responses given by women:
75 to 83%.

And an avoidance of *elle se*, especially by using *ce*, *ceux*, *on se*, or the
infinitive (for example, *se reconnaître*, to recognize oneself/each other).[6]

Ennui-lui-dire.[7]

It is very revealing that *lui*, which is ambiguous in French, is
disambiguated as *il* and not *elle*.

Je-lui (I-him/her)

Lui is disambiguated as *il* by 75% of women.
Over 85% of men chose to interpret *lui* as *il*.

Elle-lui (She-him/her)

Lui is disambiguated as *il* by 80.5% of women.

Over 85% of men interpreted *lui* as *il*.

Il(s) s'aime(nt), elle(s) s'aime(nt)—He/they [masc.] love(s)
himself/themselves or they [masc.] love each other; she/they [fem.]
love(s) herself/themselves or they [them] love each other.[8]
For the cue, *il(s) s'aime(nt)*, these were the types of response given:

> two people love one another
> a woman and a man love one another
> the lovers love one another

by both women and men. However, women's responses place more
emphasis on subjects while in men's it is on the predicate (see the
discussion of, *il(s) se parle(nt)* in the following chapter).

For the cue, *elle(s) s'aime(nt)*, the responses are different:

– many utterances, in some cases 50% of them, are of this kind: *elle(s)
sème(nt) du blé ou la pagaille*[9]—most of them use the singular:
– if the response does show a relation between two women, it is often
given a negative connotation, especially by men: *elles s'aiment les lesbiennes*,
(they love each other/ themselves—the lesbians), *elles s'aiment les salopes*
(they love each other/themselves—the bitches)...
– a fairly small percentage of women's responses indicate a family
relation, such as between mother and daughter;
– some groups of women surveyed give a relatively high number of
responses which mean: *elles s'apprécient mutuellement*, (they respect one
another) and even, *elle s'apprécie elle-même* (she respects herself).

It is surprising that *il(s)* is privileged and *elle(s)* avoided, especially by
women. For the little girl is in a privileged position regarding the
feminine gender: she is *she*, born of *she*, and her first intersubjective
relation is *between elle(s)* (them), mother and daughter.

But, during this time, the little girl is I_{she} / you_{she}. There is still no
objective representation of either of them: girl-she, mother-she or She,
and any possibility of such a designation by the feminine gender is

diminished in the mixed-sex situation of the family.

The examples of sentences a little girl addresses to her mother (whether real or imagined by women responding to linguistic tests), reveal that the daughter seeks dialogue, that she desires and asks to do or be together. These messages are evidence of respect for the two persons in speech, action or presence. Whether at the level of utterance or the level of enunciation, the two is always maintained, especially in the interrogative form of discourse that allows the mother to speak:

> *Maman, tu veux jouer avec moi?*
> (Mommy, do you want to play with me?)
> *Maman, je peux te coiffer?*
> (Mommy, can I do your hair?)

As for the mother, consideration for two persons is less obvious. The imperative takes over from the interrogative, the relation becomes hierarchical and not dialogic.

> *Rapporte-moi du lait en rentrant de l'école.*
> (Bring me some milk on your way home from school.
> *Range tes affaires avant de regarder la télé.*
> (Tidy your things before watching the T.V.)

Thus, considered as a partner in presence, in action and especially discourse, the little girl is already denied by her mother as an I$_{she}$. The mother does not speak in the same way to or of a boy as to or of a girl. In sentences produced from the cue "child," women show more respect for the other than for those formed using the word "girl."

But the little girl will also be denied or erased as *she* or *they* (*elles*) by the society or culture which force the world of *he*, *He*, *they* (*ils*), upon her; this occurs in the family, but it will be intensified from the time she goes to school. No one teaches her, in our tradition, to valorize the *she*, *She*, *they* (*elles*).

The position of the little girl, and particularly the position of her speech, relative to her mother can be schematized in the following way:

$(I_{she}) I_{she} \longrightarrow you_{she}? (you_{she})$[10]

The mother's position, in speech particularly, relative to the daughter, may be presented as:

$(I_{she}) I_{she} \longrightarrow you_{she} (\cancel{you_{she}})$

The little girl is erased as a real partner of enunciation (you_{she}) by the imperative, for example. The schema of her position thus becomes:

$(\cancel{I_{she}}) I_{she} \longrightarrow You_{she} (You_{she})$

From the moment she leaves the circle of the family (and even prior to that), from the moment she goes out into this patriarchal world of ours, the you_{she} or the You_{she} addressed to the mother will be transformed into you_{he} and especially You_{he}, with men guaranteeing the authoritarian representation of the order of speech and of culture.

These changes in the gender and nature of the partner in discourse, in presence, in action—particularly at the moment when a potential multiplicity of *you* emerges—reduce the female identity of the girl. The schema of her position in dialogue can thus be figured as:

$(I_{she}?) I_{she}? \longrightarrow you_{he} (You_{he})$

which is to become:

$I_{one} \longrightarrow you_{he}$ or You_{he}
$I_{one} \longrightarrow he$
$I_{one} \longrightarrow He$
$I_{one} \longrightarrow they$ (*ils*)

Only male subjects remain to guarantee the order of speech and culture (even if they do not assume or recognize their gender), along with a depersonalized, impersonalized female subject.

The little girl, who in speech and in the relation with the other prefers the act of dialogue, of being or doing together, is evicted from her position as communicating subject. Ever after woman will seek to recreate this context of intersubjective relations. She will only be returned to this situation of I_{she} and you_{she} by the maternal function. But this I_{she} is no longer a subject who engages in dialogue with her gender. The woman-mother orders her daughter around and subjugates her just as she is ordered around by and subjugated in the cultural universe.

The relation between two persons, which was, so to speak, co-natural to the feminine, becomes a process that has to be reconquered. Woman has to seek out the values of exchange and communication, as does man, but for different reasons. He has to overcome the priority he gives to the accumulation, possession, or at best the exchange of objects, while she must avoid the risks of hierarchy and submission, of fusion between persons, of losing her identity in the impersonality of *one*. Nevertheless exchange between persons, independent of any object, remains her objective, in spite of the obstacles she faces in her alienation of a world of *he/they* (*il(s)*) and *He* and in her symbolic preference for the other gender, which man does not always share. Is this because he lacks a sublimation of his sexed nature? Because of his practice of using woman without exchanging with her?

For centuries, in fact, woman—virgin, lover, mother—has functioned as a use-value for man and society without being a partner in exchanges. A tradition like that is not overcome in a few years or by simple decision-making. But by giving consideration to law and to language, especially the fact of their generic representation, we can bring about the evolution of division of roles between men and women, and thus modify the value of *she/they* (*elle(s)*) both as *she/they* (*elle(s)*) and in relations with *he/they* (*il(s)*).[11]

Notes

1. In this and the following chapter, I have decided to retain much of the French given that they deal with linguistic research undertaken in the French language and give an analysis of this, on the whole, strictly pertaining to French. For an analysis of similar research into North American English, see *Sexes et Genres à travers les langues* (ed. Irigaray, Grasset: 1990, English trans. Gail Schwab, forthcoming from Routledge). For an expla-

nation of *il(s)* and *elle(s)*, see note 2, p. 68 (Tr.)

2. *Chien* (dog) is a masculine noun. (Tr.)

3. *Enfant* (child) is also a masculine noun. (Tr.)

4. *Se* ("self") is the reflexive object-pronoun for the masculine and feminine third-person singular and plural, and for the impersonal *on* (one). It is used to form the infinitive of reflexive verbs, i.e. verbs expressing a reflexive action, such as *se blesser* (to hurt oneself), *se voir* (to see oneself). Reflexive verbs may be used in French in cases where the reflexive idea is either not always explicit in English (e.g. *s'habiller*, to dress (oneself)) or where English does not consider the action to be reflexive (e.g. (*se fâcher*, to get angry). They are also used as one form of constructing the passive in French (in which the subject of the sentence is not active but is given as the recipient of the action). Hence, *elle se voit* may translate as "she sees herself," or as the passive, "she is/can be seen." With more than one subject reflexive verbs may express either a reflexive action or a reciprocal one, so that, *se voir* translates as "to see oneself" and/or "to see each other" and, *elles se voient* as, "they [fem.] see themselves" and/or "each other." More figurative translations of the verb *se voir* include, to stand out, to happen/occur, to show and to find oneself. *Robe* (dress) is a feminine noun. (Tr.)

5. See above, note 4. (Tr.)

6. *Ce* is the singular demonstrative adjective, "this," and as such is masculine. As a singular demonstrative pronoun, it is neuter. *Ceux* is the plural demonstrative pronoun, "those," or "the ones," and may be a masculine or mixed-gender plural. Without some further indication of linguistic context, they cannot be distinguished, actually or orally, from *se*. *On* is the impersonal, "one." (Tr.)

7. *Ennui* is a masculine noun meaning boredom, difficulty, trouble. *Lui* is masculine/neuter used as a disjunctive personal pronoun, (him, it), and as an emphatic subject (he, it), but as an indirect object may be masculine/neuter or feminine (him, it, her); in the latter case it precedes the verb. Thus the word order here implies its use as an indirect object, whereby it could equally be masculine or feminine. *Dire* is the infinitive of the verb, to say or tell. (Tr.)

8. Without some further indication of linguistic context, the third person singular and plural cannot be distinguished orally or aurally, hence the ambiguity. (Tr.)

~

9. Whether in the third-person singular or plural, *elle(s) sème(nt)* cannot be distinguished from *elle(s) s'aime(nt)* aurally. *Semer* means to sow/to spread, thus the sense here is that she or she/they sows wheat or spreads (causes) chaos. (Tr.)

10. The partner or subject of enunciation is given in parentheses in order to distinguish him or her from the partner or subject of the utterance. (Tr.)

11. Cf. "*Le marché des femmes*" and "*Des marchandises entre elles*" in *Ce sexe qui n'en est pas un*, (Minuit: Paris, 1977), trans. " Women on the market" and "When the goods get together" in "*This Sex Which Is Not One*, trans. Catharine Porter (Cornell: Ithaca, 1985).

~ 7 ~

Two of Us, Outside, Tomorrow?

Two of us, outside, tomorrow?
I wonder where and when.
With you when?
Still need to know what to do and how.
Together perhaps?
Together everything is possible, but the others....
I'll call you to speak to you.
To speak to one another? To her!
See you soon.
Perhaps I could have thought of something else.

The exchange (?) above schematizes, on the basis of statements taken from this chapter, the normal way women and men relate and speak to one another. It makes apparent the misunderstanding between the sexes, at least as far as the linguistic factors in question are concerned.

Men and women do not produce the same sentences with the cue words *je...te* (*I...you*), *je...lui* (*I...him/her*), *elle...lui* (*she...him/her*).[1]

Men and women do not use these prepositions in the same way: *à* (to), *entre* (between), *avec* (with)—nor these adverbs: *ensemble* (together), *peut-être* (perhaps).

Men and women do not privilege the same relation to temporality.

Their responses to the instruction to make up a statement equivalent to *il(s) se parle (nt)*[2] (he/they [masc.] speak(s) to himself/themselves, or they speak to each other) and to produce a sentence with the pronouns *il* (he)...*elle* (she), are evidence of relatively explicit divergences in their use of language and in the representation they each make of their own and the other's gender.

The results used in this chapter are from the responses of different population samples, the principal ones being:

– the people attending my seminar at the International College of Philosophy over the last three years

– students from the suburbs of Paris or from the provinces questioned by their linguistics teachers (Danielle Leeman, University of Paris-X, human sciences and communications, DEUG, second year, and the first-year linguistics course, 1990; Claire Fondet, University of Burgundy, second year in literature, 1989)

– a group of people from various socio-cultural backgrounds, living in the provinces, questioned by me orally

The cue was usually given orally in order to retain the ambiguity of its meaning, and the response was usually written (except for the third group). However, as those attending my course were not all Franco-phones, I wrote the cues on the board for Group 1, indicating the possibility of a choice: *il(s) se parle(nt)*, for example.

The results of the analysis derive from 250 responses given by women, except for the cue-words *avec* (with), *entre* (between), *à* (to), *ensemble* (together), and *peut-être* (perhaps), which I have presented only to those in my seminar this year (50 responses). There are approximately 100 responses from men, except for the words noted above (20 to 30 responses depending on the cue).

The examples cited are generally from the responses given by those on my course because I wished to comment upon their own response to them directly. The results from other groups questioned have served as control groups.

The results obtained for the first cue reveal the fact that women seek communication with the other, the other-man in particular, whereas men do not. In various ways, responses to the following cues manifest the same tendency: a desire for communication on the part of women to which men do not respond since they are concerned with other things than intersubjective exchanges.

Thus, asked to make up a simple statement integrating the pronouns, *je...te* (*I...you* (direct/indirect object)) the verbs women use most frequently are:

— either *parler* (to speak), *demander* (to ask), *jurer* (to swear/to assure), *pardonner* (to forgive/pardon), *promettre* (to promise), *donner* (to give), *prévenir* (to warn), *répéter* (to repeat)—verbs expressing a situation of indirect communication: there are two persons and an explicit or implicit site of exchange between them. For example, *Je te pardonne* (I forgive you) assumes a third term between the one and the other, even if what is forgiven is not expressed. The same goes for: *Je te parle* (I talk to you), or, *je ne peux pas te parler* (I cannot talk to you).

— or *aimer* (to love), *mépriser* (to scorn), *rechercher* (to seek), *regarder* (to look/to watch), *voir* (to see), *tenir dans ses bras* (to hold in one's arms), *câliner* (to cuddle), *attendre* (to wait for)—verbs which also put two persons in relation to one another, and not a person with a thing, as generally happens in men's expressions.

It is important to note, however, that the relation of indirect communication with a man is often presented as beset with almost insurmountable difficulties:

Je ne peux pas te parler.
(I cannot talk to you.)
Je voudrais bien ne pas le répéter encore.
(I will not repeat it again.)
Je voudrais bien te le demander.
(That is something I'd like to ask you.)

Sentences are generally of this kind: *Je t'aime pour toujours mais je ne peux pas te parler.* (I'll always love you but I cannot talk to you).

In spite of this, the other in communication remains a man in many responses. When the ambiguity as to the gender of *te* is disambiguated, one third choose the feminine and two-thirds the masculine. But many other sentences show by one means or another that the *te* is masculine. As this option is more in line with the norm, it is not indicated explicitly.

The cue-words *je…te* do however offer more chance of a feminine partner than these: *je…lui* (I…him/her); *il…elle* (he…she); *ils se parlent* (they [masc.] speak to each other or to themselves), etc. When the other of communication is a woman, the relation is often direct, imagined to be one between women lovers, for example. The lack of culture in the feminine results in the fact that the relationship between women is thought of within the immediacy of love rather than within social relations and with cultural mediations. Nevertheless, there are some sentences in which an indirect relation is expressed between two women, but these are few in number. Besides, they are often anomalous in one way or another. And so the sentences: *je te la donne*, (I am giving you her/it), *Je te préviens* (I warn you) do show an intransitive communication between two women but they are incomplete and, as far as the second is concerned, it is undoubtedly an idiomatic expression as in the response: *je te promets, je suis lente* (I promise you, I am slow) (to Luce Irigaray, in response to the question: to whom is this sentence addressed). The other sentences are: *je te câline*, (I am cuddling you), *Je veux te tenir dans mes bras* (I want to hold you in my arms).

Thus, utterances expressing a relation with a man have more recourse to intransitivity, but the communication often turns out to be a failed attempt.

Men's responses indicate that the *te* is either a woman, an anonymous person, or the Other:

Je te l'avais bien dit qu'il allait neiger (à n'importe qui).
(I did tell you it was going to snow.) [to anyone])
Je te vois! (le te represente la mere d'une fille)
(I can see you! [you being a girl's mother])
Pourrais-je le faire sans ta permission? (à l'Autre)
(May I do it without your permission? [to the Other]).

In the utterances formed in response to the cue to integrate the pronouns *je…lui* (I…him/her) in a simple sentence, 90.5% of women disambiguated *lui* to be masculine. There was only one response that indicated the feminine, a response given by a person working on the sexuation of language and discourse and who uses language very carefully. Two people left *lui* ambiguous, but the context suggested that the pronoun referred to a masculine subject.

In these utterances, the verbs used often manifest communication: *dire* (to say/tell), *demander* (to ask), *parler* (to speak/talk), *téléphoner* (to telephone), *promettre* (to promise), *expliquer* (to explain). Exchange is not always possible, realizable, or accomplished but is always sought. And so there are many negative propositions, conditionals or modals: *vouloir* (to want/wish), (without being able to). The others express, as was the case for *je...te*, a relation between:

> *Je pense à lui*
> I think of him.
> *Je prends soin de lui.*
> I take care of him.
> *Je lui donne un petit cadeau.*
> I am giving him/her a small present.

Sixty percent of men—a smaller group whose results correlate to those obtained for other samples—disambiguated *lui* as *il* (the "friend" or "buddy" of *je*, usually). In 40% of the responses, *lui* is disambiguated as *elle* but the relation is an indirect one in which *je-homme* (I-man) remains the principal subject or the principal player: *Je lui ai donné beaucoup de livres et elle me les rend toujours* (I have given her lots of books and she always gives them back to me). The relation between *je* and *lui* is given in the utterance of an utterance, in a narrative, an interpolated clause, or a quotation. There are no expressions of a relation of direct communication, even between men.

In the sentences women created from the pronouns *elle* and *lui*, there is nearly always an expression of a relation between two persons (*lui* being disambiguated as a man in 85% of them, usually in the context of a couple):

— either, by way of an explicit and current relation of communication: *dire à* (to say to), *crier à* (to cry/to shout at), *s'adresser à* (to address [oneself] to), *parler à*, (to speak/talk to...)
— or, by way of a more implicit relation: *penser à* (to think of), *avoir*

confiance en (to have confidence in), *donner son temps à* (to give one's time to), *demander d'écouter* (to ask to listen)...

— or, in the form of gestures which indicate exchange is sought: *sourire à* (to smile at), *montrer le chemin à* (to show [someone] the way), *tendre la main à* (to hold one's hand out to)....

The majority of relationships expressed are thus symbolic relationships in the strict sense: there are two persons and a relation between them. The symbol is not found in an object; it is in the act of communication itself. It is symbolic to respect the fact that there are two persons and an exchange between them. The object is not indispensable.

It is quite rare for an object to be designated in these sentences, and when it is it sometimes signifies a mimetic attitude, either explicitly or implicitly:

> *Elle aussi lui rend ses clés.*
> (She also gives him/her his/her keys back)
> *Elle lui doit beaucoup d'argent*
> (She owes him/her a lot of money)
> *Elle lui fait un cadeau.*
> (She gives him/her a present)
> *Elle lui arrache les cheveux et les ongles.*
> (She tears his/her hair and nails out).

The relationship expressed is usually an indirect one: *à lui* (to him) (80.5%). To be sure, this is induced by *lui*. But it could be a question of doing something *avec lui* (with him) or *pour lui* (for him), for example. But these options would diminish the situation of communication and it is this which is privileged.

Other instances are:

— the emphatic, *Elle mangeait, lui pas*
(She was eating, *he* was not).9.5%
— *en lui* (in him)3.25%
— *de lui* (of/from him)3.25%
— *et lui* (and him)3.25%

To be sure, communication does not always seem a foregone conclusion:

> *Elle lui a crié: tais-toi.*
> (She shouted at him/her: shut up.)
> *Elle s'acharne à lui dire pourquoi.*
> (She is desperately trying to explain why to him/her.)
> *Elle lui a dit d'écouter.*
> (She told him/her to listen).
> *Elle ne pouvait pas lui sourire.*
> (She couldn't smile at him/her.)
> *Elle ne lui a pas dit....*
> (She did not tell him/her....)

Yet communication is sought.

When it comes to the prevalence of *à* (marking intransitivity or indirection) in the relation of communication, it is significant that in response to the cue to make a sentence with the preposition *à*, 27% of women use the forms: *à lui* (to him), *à toi* (to you), *à l'autre* (to the other).

Men's sentences do not contain this use of *à* manifesting exchange between (two) persons. Rather, they use the *à* in the following ways:

> *J'habite à Paris*
> (I live in Paris)
> *Nous sommes allés à la ville*
> (We went into town)
> *J'ai quelque chose à dire*
> (I have something to say)
> *Elle a à construire*
> (She has to build)
> *Je viens à apprendre*
> (I come to learn)

Similarly, with the cue *entre* (between/among), 65% of women form an utterance that puts two or more persons in relation to one another:

Il y a une atmosphère de grande curiosité entre nous.
(There is an atmosphere of intense curiosity among us.)
L'écart entre lui et elle était infime.
(The distance between him and her was very slight.)
Nous sommes entre amis.
(We are among friends.)

Fifty-eight percent of men use this meaning of *entre*, but more than half of their responses give an indication of the negative character of the relation expressed:

Entre toi et moi, une distance si froide.
(There is such coolness between you and I.)
Il y a des problèmes entre nous.
(There are problems between us.)

or they eliminate difference:

Il n'y a pas de différence entre un Néerlandais et un Hollandais.
(There is no difference between someone from the Netherlands and someone from Holland.)
Entre est dans.
(Between is within.)
Entre sans frapper, c'est entre nous.
(Enter without knocking, there're no formalities between us.)

This is not true in women's responses, where difference always expresses a space between, a space that is generally positively valorized.

Another interesting distinction arises. Women do sometimes speak of one between me and me, a meaning not given by men at all. The same goes for this meaning: *au milieu de* (in the middle of/among).

In response to the request to make a sentence using the preposition *avec* (with), 50% of women's responses stage a relation between two persons. The other choices express a felt condition: with difficulty, with pleasure, with joy, with interest, with my solitude or, in a few rare cases, a meaning such as: with a ball-point pen, with the weather.

Of the sentences created by men, 30.5% stage two persons in a relation, yet it is either through the mediation of a concept or an abstract operation (with the assistance of), or there is some equivocation as to the existence of the two, or some perplexity (*Avec qui, je me demande, dois-je marcher?* (Who should I walk with, I wonder?), or it negates a relation.

Men's responses use the preposition *avec* more in the sense of 'by means of'; 31% do this. A few of the utterances express a felt condition. In two sentences, *avec* signifies accompaniment by a person or it is used almost instrumentally: *avec le vent* (with the wind).

In response to the cue to make a statement equivalent to *il(s) se parle(nt)*[3], a cue given orally and left ambiguous as to its possible signification, women's sentences designate the following subjects:

two persons	43%
ils + a verb of communication (but this *ils* is generally two persons)	45.5%
he talks to himself	2.2%
there is between them	2.2%
noun without a verb	2.2%

The verbs used often express communication: they exchange; they dialogue; they communicate; two persons communicate orally; two persons hold a conversation; two persons discuss; they speak to one another; two persons listen to one another. In addition to verbs expressing communication, the relation is manifested by prepositions, adverbs, substantives: between them, mutually, to exchange news, complicity, reconciliation, conversation, discussion.

Use of the masculine as generic is so overwhelming that even the word *personnes*[4] is pronominalized as if it were *ils*: *Des personnes communiquent entre eux,* (Two persons communicate among themselves) or, *Ils communiquent entre eux* (They communicate among themselves—two or more persons).

There are no sentences with a negative connotation. To be sure, the emphasis is often upon the discussion but surely this is to emphasize the two rather than the negative. This interpretation is supported by the context.

~

The characteristics of men's responses are different.

The act of speaking is banalized, as it were, through the context: *Les gens se parlent dans la rue* (People speak to one another in the street), *Les gens se parlent* (People speak to one another).

— There are a few indications to suggest that it is a question of a relation between, of communication between, of dialogue.

— There are few sentences indicating the involvement of two persons.

— There are lots of sentences of the type: *Il se parle à lui-même*, (he talks to himself), often with added comments along the lines of: the madman, a loner, a silent individual, old Narcissus in love with himself, homosexuality (25% of the responses were like this in some groups questioned).

With reference to specifications that were made, we find:

— few indications are given as to *who* is speaking;

— some indications as to *what* they are talking about: *Ils se parlent d'amour* (They are talking about love), *Ils se parlent de choses et d'autres* (They are talking about just anything);

— most of the additions or specifications are about *how* they are speaking: in French, with warmth like two old friends; very little; at length before taking action; quietly, whispering, and *where il(s) se parle(nt)*: in the street, in closed session, through the counter window.

— the context suggests that two men or a group of men are spoken of; when the gender is given, it is masculine; there is no suggestion of mixed-sex situations, no sentence indicating the presence of women.

Women's responses to the cue to make a sentence with the pronouns *il* and *elle* are fairly indicative of the paucity of real or symbolic relations between women and men, even though they are sought.

— No *il* or *elle* was taken to be in the plural.

— *Elle* and *il* are situated in two different clauses; this is obviously implied by the cue presented which gives two possible subjects to make one sentence. But placing them in the same clause was not out of the question. For example: *Il vient avec elle ce soir* (He is coming with her tonight), *Il part sans elle* (He leaves without her), *Il va se marier avec elle* (He is going to marry her), *Il(s) parle(nt) d'elle* (He/They is/are talking about her), etc.[5] The representation of the feminine as *elle* is difficult in the form of a subject but even more so as a complement, since this assumes a confirmation of the identity or identification of the feminine as belonging to the feminine gender. While woman, women, are not used to saying *je*, they are even less accustomed to saying *elle(s)*, and do not imagine constituting themselves as feminine partners of *il*. The types of response given to this cue are similar to those given for *ennui-lui-dire, je-lui,* and *elle-lui*.

   — *Elle* and *il* are, in women's sentences, human animates.

   — In women's sentences, *elle* and *il* generally desigante loving partners, indeed sexual ones in the strict sense of the term: her husband, a couple, again the boyfriend, John, (as partner), the (male) friend of a (female) friend, the ex-lover, the husband, or her boyfriend, David. The other remaining choices are genealogical: the girl and her grandfather, her son, a girl and her father.

   — The order reproduced in the response is that given in the cue: *elle-il*.

It is interesting to look at the kind of relations imagined between *elle* and *il*:

   Actions are contrapuntal, juxtaposed, almost antagonistic:

> *Elle parle, il chante* (She is talking; he is singing)
>
> *Elle souriait, il parlait* (She was smiling; he was talking)
>
> *Elle à regardé le coucher de soleil pendant qu'il fronçait le sourcil* (She watched the sunset while he frowned)
>
> *Il mange, elle regarde* (He is eating; she is watching)

The predicates are openly conflictual:

> *Elle la veut, lui non.*
>
> (She wants it, he does not.)
>
> *Elle adore de sortir tandis que lui n'aime pas trop.*
>
> (She loves to go out whereas he is not so keen to do so.)

~

Elle n'aime pas qu'il reste dans la maison.
(She does not like him to stay at home.)
Elle ne veut pas qu'il vienne.
(She does not want him to come.)
Elle est partie avant qu'il la quitte.
(She left before he leaves her.)
Cette femme est formidable tandis que lui est méprisable.
(That woman is great whereas he is despicable.)
Elle ne va pas bien, il ne voit rien.
(She is not well and he cannot see it.)

What is expressed manifests a misunderstanding, a fear of incomprehension, or some trust that has been broken:

Elle ne sait pas trop s'il est malade, mais il l'est.
(She is not quite sure if he is ill, but he is.)
Elle croyait qu'il avait été sincère.
(She thought he had been true.)
Elle a peur qu'il ne réponde pas.
(She is afraid he will not reply.)

Responses show a positive relation, a situation that is rare and often intra-familial:

Elle lui a dit qu'il était intelligent (à son fils).
(She told him he was intelligent [her son].)
Elle veut qu'il arrive (fille et pere).
(She wants him to arrive [daughter and father].)

Sentences refer to a meeting without being precise as to the connotations of that meeting:

Elle et il se recontrent au café (Marie et Jean).
(She and he meet up at the café.)
Il pense à elle (Y et X).
(He thinks about her.)

There are, therefore, no actions undertaken simultaneously, together, or with, nor even coordinated actions. Very often, the negative character of the relation is shown, either explicitly or implicitly. The only positive relations are family ones and the positiveness is unilateral, on the part of *she* in relation to her son or her father. If the question of subordination between the action of *he* and *she* arises, this is accompanied by doubt, fear, and enforced tolerance; nothing favorable is connoted.

These responses somewhat contradict many of the responses given by women which postulate a positive relation with a man. There are several reasons for this, notably the use of *she* and the difficulty of a truly intersubjective relation between *he* and *she*. This factor emerges in other sets of responses, particularly the sentences made with *robe-se-voir* and *ennui-lui-dire*.[6] Nevertheless, the responses to the cues *je-te* and *je-lui* show less evidence of the impossibility of a relation between *elle* and *lui*. It is true, however, that here the woman expresses herself as *I* and not as *she*.

Men's responses (from a smaller corpus) show similar tendencies to those found in the analysis of women's responses: no plurals, the situation of *he* and *she* in different clauses, the contraposition, indeed opposition between the actions or speech of *he* and *she*.

There are nevertheless several differences which should be noted:

— There is a greater emphasis on the object or the objective:

> *Elle aime tout ce qu'il fait.*
> (She likes everything he does.)
> *Elle aime le vin rouge tandis qu'il préfère le blanc.*
> (She likes red wine whereas he prefers white.)
> *Il le voit mais elle ne le voit pas encore.*
> (He can see him/it but she cannot yet.)

— The superiority of the masculine is sometimes clearly affirmed, even through supposedly feminine intentions or choices:

> *Elle aime tout ce qu'il fait.*
> (She likes everything he does.)

Il le voit mais elle ne le voit pas encore.
(He can see him/it but she cannot yet.)

— Sometimes the man's indifference to the woman is openly expressed:

Elle lui demande, il s'en fout!
(She asks him but he doesn't give a damn!)
Il se sent bien, elle pleure.
(He feels fine; she is crying.) (suggesting perplexity? L.I.)

— One response is erotic, manifesting the authority of *il* over *elle*:

Il veut faire l'amour avec elle.
(He wants to make love with her.)

— There are some sentences (particularly from people engaged in this research) in which the possibility of another mode of communication seems to be emerging:

Il lui demande ce qu'elle pense.
(He asks her what she thinks.)
Elle et il s'aiment.
(She and he love one another.)

The difference between what women hope for as communicative relation and the actual reality is also marked by responses to the word *ensemble* (together). Curiously, in response to this men use persons as the subject more than women (87.5% out of a small sample). However, the togetherness is indeterminate, and even restricted:

Ensemble, tout est possible.
(Together, everything is possible.)
Oui, d'accord nous sommes ensemble.
(Yes, OK, we are together.)
Nous allons passer quelque temps ensemble.
(We are going to spend some time together.)

On n'y va pas ensemble.
(We are not going together.)

Another surprising result was that 25% of the responses give *elles* as the subject:

Elles arrivèrent ensemble au cours.
(They arrived together in class.)
Elles devraient y aller ensemble.
(They ought to go together.)

Of course, women still use the person as subject a good deal. This is true for 60% of the sentences produced, although one third of these responses manifest difficulties, doubts, pejorative nuances or negative transformations, which are normally unusual in the language women use. A further third of the statements seem to report the possibility of being together in the future, sometimes in the form of an injunction. *Allons ensemble voir ta grand-mère* (Let's go to see your grandmother together). Another surprising result was that *ensemble* was used as a substantive in a quarter of the responses,[7] and so the question of persons being together was avoided. While women hope to be with, to be together, this does not always seem to go without saying and sometimes they use strategies to avoid broaching the issue of the difficulty of being together. As is often the case, women's responses speak more of a concrete being together, frequently for two. Men's responses signify a much vaguer being together, more collective and indeterminate. It seems to me that for them this being together often entails a loss of individuation. While woman, women, lose their female identity in the mixed-sex *ils* or in the generic *il*, men seem to abdicate their personality in the collectivity of a rather indeterminate sociality, a sort of *one*, or one + one + one… uniting their members for its purposes without constituting relations between persons.

The use of the *past tense* is more in evidence in men's utterances, at least in French. Often their discourse stretches between present and past, and is almost regressive. Their certitudes or points of anchorage are generally situated in the past. Reference to the past tense may be expressed through already existing definitions of a truth, concept, or reality.

Women produce utterances which are more related to the *current context* or open to the *future*. Such a use of the future often reveals a desire for communication. It also relates to the frequency of allusions to displacements in space and to what the weather will be like. This cosmic component plays a greater part in women's discourse than in that of men, even in an artificially created situation, as when taking part in research into the way language is used.

By asking participants to make a sentence incorporating the adverb *peut-être* (perhaps), my intention was to see how women and men would deploy this modality, especially in relation to temporality.

In women's responses, 64% use *peut-être* with a future reference, whereas only 25% of men's responses did this. Among the women, the adverb thus serves to suggest a future possibility: among men, on the other hand, it expresses uncertainty concerning the nature of the object or the intention of the other in relation to oneself, or doubt regarding what one has accomplished:

> *Peut-être ce bruit-là est-il une musique.*
> (Perhaps some would call that noise music.)
> *Elle l'aime peut-être.*
> (Perhaps she loves him.)
> *Peut-être aurais-je pu penser autre chose.*
> (Perhaps I could have thought of something else.)

This kind of response is not to be found in any of the responses given by women. Rather, one finds the following:

> *Peut-être irai-je voir mon amie chez elle.*
> (Perhaps I will go to my friend's house to see her.)
> *Peut-être viendra-t-il un enfant dans cette maison.*
> (Perhaps there will be a child in this house.)
> *Peut-être va-t-il pleuvoir.*
> (Perhaps it is going to rain.)
> *Peut-être qu'un jour je pourrai faire comme si....*
> (One day, perhaps, I will be able to imagine....)

Elle viendra peut-être avec moi.
(Perhaps she will come with me.)

The last response, using *elle* in the subject position, was produced by a woman who is aware of language use since she has undertaken research in German as a member of an international research group formed to look at "Sexual Difference and Communication(s)".

Following the analysis of the responses, the tendencies found may be summarized as following:

— Women seek communication, especially dialogue, but they particularly address themselves to *lui/il* (him/he) whose interest is not intersubjective exchange and who is more oriented towards the past than towards the present or the future;

— Men are interested in the concrete object if it is theirs (my car, my watch, my pipe, etc.), or in the abstract object insofar as it is proper to a man or sanctioned by the already existing community of men, their psychological states, or their genealogical and familial problems; they rarely seek dialogue and remain within a collectivity that is poorly defined but marked by the masculine gender.

Notes

1. For an explanation of *lui*, see note 7, p. 77. (Tr.)
2. Again, the third person singular and plural cannot be differentiated orally or aurally. (Tr.)
3. See above, note 2. (Tr.)
4. *Personnes* is a feminine noun, but the corresponding personal pronoun is given as *eux*, the masculine *themselves*, rather than the feminine, *elles*. (Tr.)
5. *Elle* is used for both the subject pronoun, 'she,' or 'it,' and the disjunctive pronoun, 'her.' (Tr.)
6. With reference to this, see *Sexes et genres à travers les langues*, op. cit.
7. As a noun *ensemble* may mean unity, a whole, a set or an outfit (to wear). (Tr.)

~ 8 ~

He I Sought But Did Not Find

Relationships between people, and the desire for and use of communication, are more typical of women, as I have shown in numerous examples. Yet, these interpersonal relations are deprived of sexed identity, of I_{she} and of relations to one or to several partners of the same gender. In the responses given during linguistic research in various languages, few utterances make manifest a relationship between women.[1] A woman almost has to be both an active feminist, aware of her cultural alienation, and someone who has thought about her dependence upon language for her to make sentences that manage not to rule out a relation between women, although, to repeat, the percentage of sentences expressing a relation between women or a relationship of the subject of enunciation to a woman or to several women is very low, barely a few percent.

Women therefore speak unaware of their I_{she} and without communicating with a *you*$_{she}$ whether by direct or indirect communication:

I_{she} speak to you_{she}—direct communication, or, I_{she} speak about *her*—indirect communication. In those cases where it does appear, the woman's *I* is left to relations with you_{he}, *he* or *He* and to $they_{he}$ (*ils*).

In this situation—one created by culture and language—dialogue becomes difficult, indeed impossible, particularly between daughter and mother. Yet women still desire to communicate, the results of linguistic research show that. In their responses women set the stage for two people; they represent them in a situation of communication; they use many verbs, prepositions and adverbs which describe dialogue and communication—not always possible but almost always sought after. In view of this, it is quite right to say that women are the guardians of communication, even if this communication is in many ways stultified and lacking real partners at present. Women would appear to be the guardians of love not only as mothers but also as speaking subjects whose message is above all to communicate.

With the loss of their I_{she} and you_{she}, their desire or intention to communicate is almost exclusively oriented toward *he/they* (*il[s]*). Intentionality thus artificially remains turned in a privileged direction: toward *he/they*, and with no return to the female self nor between female selves. The *he/they* becomes a pseudo-transcendence to which *she* is oriented, losing her subjectivity on the way, and thus the possibility of real communication.

Communication, exchange between people, intersubjectivity—the privileged loci of the least alienated female identity—are thus held back from appropriation by the female gender and from reciprocity between the sexes. With no return to the self, woman/women cannot truly engage in dialogue. They concern themselves with men—especially fathers and sons—situate themselves in familiar surroundings, hope for the future and continually try to communicate, particularly in the form of a question that might actually be a hope of being returned to themselves through the response they receive. And so in various ways they ask: Do you love me? The question really means: What am I for you? Or, Who am I? or, How can I return to myself?

More often than not the man gives no response. And in this order romantic courtship is not really a response since the woman is desired bodily, not spiritually and energetically and in the respect for her mother, her first transcendence. Libido is masculine, or neuter, so Freud claims. Yet there is a specific feminine energy, related more to communication, to growth, and not just to reproduction. A fairly common representation of the carnal act, and again a Freudian one, presents it as an immolation of energy—especially feminine energy. Energy is to be sacrificed by man for the sake of his return to the serious matters of public life, culture, science—activities that, it would seem, need to be cleansed of every aspect of affectivity and sexuality by returning to a zero degree of libidinal tension. As far as the woman is concerned, it has to be sacrificed in order to annul her own existence and the problems she poses. Energy is not to be cultivated in accordance with two modalities, two realities or truths, two measures (in the sense of rhythm as well as rationality), two temporalities, two tonalities, two voices, two colors. It is to be sacrificed on the cross—writes Hegel—rising toward a so-called neutral truth, devoid of perceptive and sensorial qualities, an everlasting truth, alien to our bodies living in the here and now.

The Western tradition typically represents living energy as sacrificed to spirit, to a truth assimilated to immutable ideals, beyond growth, beyond corporeality; celestial ideals imposed as models so that we all become alike—our sensible, natural and historical differences neutralized.

In this sense, the demand for equality for all, between all men and all women, is indeed faithful to our secular metaphysical ideal, an ideal aimed at universality, totality, the absolute, and essence by reducing distinctions and dissimilarities. This ideal intends to neutralize the specific energy of living beings in a puppet pantomime with one master—be it profit, technology, or a civil or religious master—pulling the strings.[2]

At the other extreme of this ideal becoming—not in terms of a destiny proper to the subject but in terms of an abstract model—nature carries out its generative fertile task: woman produces children. This act is also universally idealized, not as the culture of the woman's psychological energy, but rather as the exaltation of a natural act required by the public realm. Energy is utilized, on the one hand, to transform man, the citizen, into a slave to preconceived notions and, on the other hand, to venerate procreation which in itself is but a natural act. Our tradition thus lives on in an unresolved contradiction between an abstract ideal, split off from concerns for growth and sensible qualities, and a veneration of life in its raw state. With this contradiction, the culture of energy is paralyzed and destroyed. Humanity remains suspended between the contemplation of certain natural phenomena and the marvels or disasters of technological energy without being able to manage its own human energy.

In this context, war still fascinates as a sort of energetic debauchery or potlatch. Whether the energy is engendered by living beings or is manufactured, notably by technology, there is sacrifice, killing, and destruction. Once this excessive expenditure is over, order is more or less restored on a temporary basis but nothing has actually been resolved. Energy between human beings does not operate any better, quite the opposite. War brings with it hatred, resentment, grief, and anguish, which takes years, centuries even, to redress. And the question, "Why?", always remains, a question it seems impossible to answer.

If we are to regulate and cultivate energy between human beings, we need language. But not just denotative language, language that names, declares the reality or truth of things and transmits information; we also and especially need language that facilitates and maintains communication. And it is not just the lexicon we are talking about, but a syntax appropriate to intersubjectivity. This also calls into question why we speak—the very purpose of speech.

Regarding exchange, we have seen that women seek communication and especially dialogue. This quest, which, owing to culture, language, and to some extent, desire, is especially addressed to *he/they* (*il[s]*), does not meet with reciprocity. For men's teleology implies rather an abandonment of immediate communication—of intersubjectivity and dialogue—in order to set off in quest of an *oeuvre* (in which they usually alienate themselves) and, among other things, a spiritual journey compelled by a transcendence appropriate to their ego.

Hegel clearly points to this in the development of the dialectic: the individual is estranged from natural, sensible immediacy for the sake of a spiritual becoming in which reciprocal communication is never considered a goal of spirituality. This development works through the forward projections of an in-itself that becomes for-itself through reflection. Spirit is increasingly estranged from nature and in this movement supposedly assimilates all the in-itself and spiritualizes it.

Man is only able to communicate with other men by means of mediations: in the public realm, at work, in religion and so forth. But these mediations are already *his*. Men communicate in a public realm constructed in accordance with their model of identity, in accordance with their laws. However, their culture emphasizes property and abstract ideal values rather than relations between people. The community of men is generally an aggregate of one + one + one... whose individuation is abolished in the construction of a whole defined by geography, history, language, property or capital, opinions or beliefs, leaders or representatives, either elected or imposed, and so on.

Such are the persons who make up the whole but they are no longer persons explicitly related to their generic identity, as in the family. And what's more, they do not communicate among themselves except through already codified mediations: language, law, and religion, relations which leave little room for speaking subjects in the here and now. Among themselves, men hardly say a word to each other. They talk about the incidental aspects of daily life, they argue, but they do not communicate. They pass on news, and comment upon it. The fact that we neither realize that men and women do not talk in the same way nor appreciate what the differences are between their discourses is a sign, or symptom, of the absence of communication in the public realm of men. To say that men speak more objectively, women more emotionally, proves to be very much an approximation of the truth and is, in any case, partially wrong.

On the other hand, it would seem that women do communicate more and that men use language in order to denote reality or to produce and establish their truths rather than to communicate (immediately or mediately) among themselves.

How, then, can women and men be brought together if they each follow such different intentions? I believe that the process Hegel named recognition is one means of putting them face to face with each other again, one with the other, man and woman. Recognition is the act that could enable the hierarchical domination between the sexes to be overcome, which could restore woman and man, women and men, to their respective identity and dignity, and which should bring about relations that are cultured, spiritual and not merely natural; relations founded upon a form of indirection or intransitivity. And so: I love to you, rather than: I love you.[3]

Notes

1. Cf. *Sexes et genres à travers les langues*, op. cit.
2. Plato's allegory of the cave was, during his time, a staging of such a pantomime. (cf. *Speculum of the Other Woman*).
3. Here and in the following chapters Irigaray transforms verbs in their transitive form (that is, a verb that customarily or in a given occurrence requires a direct object) into intransitive verbs (a verb not requiring a direct object). The verb *aimer*, to love or to like, is a transitive verb in French as in English. With *je t'aime* (I love you), the pronoun, *te* (you) is not only the direct object of the subject, *je* (I), but in French precedes the verb, so that the *te*, the potential other, is spatially 'assimilated' between the subject and his/her action. Irigaray intends the other to be positioned as subject not object, thus 'you' (*toi*) is not to be considered an indirect object of the verb as such. Introducing the preposition *à* syntactically separates the 'you' (*toi*) from the action of the 'I', and is intended to suggest a movement towards the other subject rather than the constitution of this latter by the action of the 'I'. Thus, *j'aime à toi*. I have chosen to translate *à* as 'to,' since I consider it best conveys this sense of movement towards the other as subject while not deviating from the relative simplicity of the transformed grammatical structure in French. Except where explicitly stated, the *à toi, à moi*, etc., although used as possessive pronouns in French (yours, mine), are not intended to function as such here.

~ 9 ~

You Who Will Never Be Mine

How are we to outline the process of recognition?

I recognize you, thus you are not the whole; otherwise you would be too great and I would be engulfed by your greatness. You are not the whole and I am not the whole.

I recognize you, thus I may not revolve around you, I cannot encircle you or introject you. You are not an *illic* that can become a *hic*, to use Husserl's terminology. I cannot completely identify you, even less identify with you.

I recognize you means that I cannot know you in thought or in flesh. The power of a negative prevails between us. I recognize you goes hand in hand with: you are irreducible to me, just as I am to you. We may not be substituted for one another. You are transcendent to me, inaccessible in a way, not only as ontic being but also as ontological being (which entails, in my view, fidelity to life rather than submission to death).

Between us there is always transcendence, not as an abstraction or a construct, a fabrication of the same grounding its origin or measuring its development, but as the resistance of a concrete and ideational reality: I will never be you, either in body or in thought.

Recognizing you means or implies respecting you as other, accepting that I draw myself to a halt before you as before something insurmountable, a mystery, a freedom that will never be mine, a subjectivity that will never be mine, a mine that will never be mine.

I recognize you is the one condition for the existence of I, *you* and *we*. Nor will it ever be neuter, a collective *one*. This *we* is the work of the negative, that which cannot be substituted between us, the transcendence between us. It is constituted by subjects irreducible one to the other, each one to the others, and thus capable of communicating out of freedom and necessity. Spiritual progress can be understood, then, as the development of communication between us, in the form of individual and collective dialogue. Speech *between* replaces instinctual attraction or the attraction of similitude.

I recognize you signifies that you are different from me, that I cannot identify myself (with) nor master your becoming. I will never be your master. And it's this negative that enables me to go towards you.

I recognize you supposes that I cannot see right through you. You will never be entirely visible to me, but, thanks to that, I respect you as different from me. What I do not see of you draws me towards you provided you hold your own, and provided your energy allows me to hold my own and raise mine with you. I go towards you as towards that which I shall not see but which attracts me, like a path of becoming, of progress. This progress does not mean estrangement from flesh, from my body, from my history. I go towards that which enables me to become while remaining myself.

Transcendence is thus no longer ecstasy, leaving the self behind toward an inaccessible total-other, beyond sensibility, beyond the earth. It is respect for the other whom I will never be, who is transcendent to me and to whom I am transcendent. Neither simple nature nor common spirit beyond nature, this transcendence exists in the difference of body and culture that continues to nourish our energy, its movement, its generation and its creation. Our energy is thence no longer channelled, sublimated, or paralyzed in a movement towards a beyond *I-me*, or *you*, or *we*. It is the movement and transformation that limits the empire of my ego, of the power of *you*, or of the community and its already established values. It remains in me, enstasy rather than ecstasy, but ready to meet with the other, particularly through language, without sacrificing sensibility.

The other of sexual difference is he—or she—towards whom it is possible to go as towards a transcendence, while remaining in the self, and without turning transcendence on its head in the guise of soul or spirit. I will never reach this other, and for that very reason, *he/she* forces me to remain in my self in order to be faithful to *him/her* and *us*, retaining our difference.

I recognize you signifies that you are, that you exist, that you become. With this recognition, I mark you, I mark myself with incompleteness, with the negative. Neither you nor I are the whole nor the same, the principle of totalization. And our difference cannot be reduced to *one* hierarchy, *one* genealogy, *one* history. It cannot be weighed in terms of more or less. That would be to annihilate it.

Recognition is the process by which Hegel's master-slave dialectic can be overcome. Yet, in the Hegelian system, this is only possible with the transition to absolute spirit, an absolute spirit in fact determined as unisex and therefore not as a concrete universal. In order to avoid master(s)/slave(s) relations, we have to practice a different sort of recognition from the one marked by hierarchy, and thus also by genealogy. Saying that the child is the death of its parents amounts to leaving spirit in a form of naturalism and to believing that History entails a sacrifice, sacrifices. Provided the child partakes of a culture concerned with communication, with intersubjectivity, with spiritualizing the difference between the sexes, then the parents may look forward to a better future society, besides the opportunity for their own development as lovers. Above all, though, the power of the one over the other will be no more. Difference that is irreducible never ceases to curb the capitalization of any such power, of mere authority over.

Only the recognition of the other as sexed offers this possibility. Between woman and man, man and woman, recognition requires the labor of the negative. Mastery of, substitution for, thereby become impossible processes given the respect for what is, for what exists.

Sexual identity resolves another risk highlighted in Adorno's work, for instance, but in other critiques of Hegel as well.[1] Sexed identity rules out all forms of totality as well as the self-substituting subject (and the *existentialia*). The *mine* of the subject is always already marked by a disappropriation: gender. Being a man or a woman already means not being the whole of the subject or of the community or of spirit, as well as not being entirely one's self. The famous *I* is another, the cause of which is sometimes attributed to the unconscious, can be understood in a different way. *I* is never simply *mine* in that it belongs to a gender. Therefore, I am not the whole: I am man or woman. And I am not simply a subject, I belong to a gender. I am objectively limited by this belonging.

The reluctance to recognize the importance of sexual difference seems to me to derive from this negative in the self and for the self it entails. I belong to a gender, which means to a sexed universal and to a relation between two universals.

In psychoanalytic theory and practice, belonging to a gender might, in part, serve as the third term in the constitution of adult identity. The imperative of the law and the power of the father are thereby rendered obsolete. It is necessary and sufficient for me to respect the gender I am. The play of the same and the other, present in generic identity, enables me to get away from dependence upon genealogy, from childhood, from incest. Thus I am engendered by two, carried by and born of a woman, nourished by her, but I am man or woman, and, as such, I must become who I am and not stay attached to an/my infantile destiny and dependency.

The obligation to belong to my gender might provide a way of reinterpreting Freud's Oedipus complex. We are not forced to choose, as he claims, between the prohibition of incest and psychosis. All we need do is become our gender in order to get away from an undifferentiated relation with the mother—assuming this form of relation is not in fact just a male fantasy.[2]

But becoming one's gender also constitutes the means for returning to the self. The self cannot enter into the realm of pure knowledge, pure understanding. Belonging to a gender cannot be known or accepted in the way the truth, the truths, of classical philosophy were. This truth is in part passivity, fidelity to the being I am, being given to me by nature and which I must endorse, respect and cultivate as one half of human identity, albeit *two*, not *one*. The being I am is thus never the whole and is always separate (from) inasmuch as it is a function of a gender. It cannot, therefore, be in a state of fusion, either in childhood or in love. Furthermore, this being is an opening to the other gender, genealogically and horizontally.

In this perspective, there is no more "natural immediacy." I am a sexed ontological or ontic being, hence assigned to a gender, to a generic identity, one which I am not necessarily in/through my sensible immediacy. And so to be born a girl in a male-dominated culture is not necessarily to be born with a sensibility appropriate to my gender. No doubt female physiology is present but not identity, which remains to be constructed. Of course, there is no question of its being constructed in repudiation of one's physiology. It is a matter of demanding a culture, of wanting and elaborating a spirituality, a subjectivity and an alterity appropriate to this gender: the female. It's not as Simone de Beauvoir said: one is not born, but rather becomes, a woman (through culture), but rather: I am born a woman, but I must still become this woman that I am by nature.

As for the "absolute spirit," the recognition of sexed identity as a dimension of a spiritual culture renders the unity of this totalization impossible. In fact, each gender must define and retain mediations appropriate to it, and we must determine mediations enabling communication and exchange between the genders. But there will be no final synthesis. There will be no definitive "negation of negation." Man being irreducible to woman and woman to man, there no longer exists any *absolute* spirit nor *one* finality of being. The relation between man and woman, men and women, takes place on the grounds of a groundless ground. It is without definitive resolution or assumption, always becoming in the outward and return journeying between one and the other, the ones and the others, with no end or final reckoning.

An intentionality has to be at work if these return journeys leading to the development of communication are to be motivated. It is necessary that *he* and *she*, I_{he} - I_{she}, and *you*$_{he}$ - *you*$_{she}$, are valued and that their relations constitute a site of rising rather than diminishing energy.

Women and men must therefore be recognized as representatives or as incarnations of human gender. They have to be valorized for the sake of the becoming of their sexed *I*, for the relations between them and for the constitution of a spiritual dialectic of these relations.

In this way, intentionality between them cannot become an obligation to reproduce nor especially an occasion for degeneracy. It must be motivated by the desire for an individual and collective spiritual becoming realized by woman and man, women and men.

For this becoming, women and men need to find ways of relating to one another and of communicating, ways avoiding the pitfalls of an unmediated being-with-the-other for the female gender, and for the male gender, of being-with-the-tool, hand, object, money, or language at the expense of intersubjectivity and of recognition of the other. We must, therefore, define a relation of indirection between the genders in which we overcome the obstacles posed by relations of appropriation or of fusion between persons and by replacing intersubjective relationships with instrumentality. The "to" in the expression "I love to you," attempts to support this double intention by confounding an inertia found in both sexes and which paralyzes exchanges between them.

Notes

1. See *The Jargon of Authenticity*, trans. Knut Tarnowski & Frederic Will, Evanston: Northwestern University Press, 1973.
2. Read, for example, the interview, "On the Maternal Order," in *Je, Tu, Nous*, op. cit.

~ 10 ~

I Love To You

I love to you means I maintain a relation of indirection to you.[1] I do not subjugate you or consume you. I respect you (as irreducible). I hail you: in you I hail. I praise you: in you I praise. I give you thanks: to you I give thanks for... I bless you. for... I speak to you, not just about something; rather I speak *to* you. I tell you, not so much this or that, but rather I tell *to* you.

The "to" is the guarantor of indirection. The "to" prevents the relation of transitivity, bereft of the other's irreducibility and potential reciprocity. The "to" maintains intransitivity between persons, between the interpersonal question, speech or gift: I speak to you, I ask of you, I give to you (and not: I give *you* to another).

The "to" is the sign of non-immediacy, of mediation between us. Thus, it is not: I order you or command you to do some particular thing, which could mean or imply: I prescribe this for you, I subject you to these truths, to this order—whether these amount to a form of labor or to a form of human or divine pleasure. Nor is it: I seduce you to me, the you becoming (what belongs) to me; the "I love to you" becoming "I love (what belongs) to me." Any more than it is: I marry you, in the sense that I am making you my wife or my husband, that is: I take you, I am making you mine. Rather, it is: I hope to be attentive to you now and in the future, I ask you if I may stay with you, and I am faithful to you.

The "to" is the site of non-reduction of the person to the object. I love you, I desire you, I take you, I seduce you, I order you, I instruct you, and so on, always risk annihilating the alterity of the other, of transforming him/her into my property, my object, of reducing him/her to what is mine, into mine, meaning what is already a part of my field of existential or material properties.

The "to" is also a barrier against alienating the other's freedom in my subjectivity, my world, my language.

I love to you thus means: I do not take you for a direct object, nor for an indirect object by revolving around you. It is, rather, around myself that I have to revolve in order to maintain the *to you* thanks to the return to me. Not with my prey—you become mine—but with the intention of respecting my nature, my history, my intentionality, while also respecting yours. Hence, I do not return to me by way of: I wonder if I am loved. That would result from an introverted intentionality, going toward the other so as to return ruminating, sadly and endlessly, over solipsistic questions in a sort of cultural cannibalism.

The "to" is the guarantor of two intentionalities: mine and yours. In you I love that which can correspond to my own intentionality and to yours.

It could be that what I love in you—"to you"—is not consciously willed by you and escapes your intentions: a certain mannerism, a particular expression, a feature of your body, your sensibility. We have to see if we can build a *we* on the basis of what, of *you*, is thus compatible with my intentions but escapes your own (less conscious as it may be for you). On the basis of this *to you*—more a property of yours than an intention, assuming this distinction holds—can we construct a temporality?

The problem of *we* is that of a meeting which occurs through fortune, good fortune, as it were (a *kairos*?), or partly that of a coincidence whose

~

necessity escapes us, but it is also or especially that of constituting a temporality: together, with, between. All too often, sacramental or juridical commitment and the obligation to reproduce have compensated for this problem: how to construct a temporality between us? How to unite two temporalities, two subjects, in a lasting way?

For making you my property, my possession, my *mine* does not accomplish the alliance between us. This act sacrifices one subjectivity to another. The "to" becomes a possessive, a sign of possession and not of an existential property. But what if it is claimed that man is a possessor who transforms his instincts into laws? In that case, the "to" of possession is no longer bilateral. You are (what belongs) to me, often without any reciprocity. In this mine that you are, you lose the freedom of reciprocity; never mind the fact that the possessor is scarcely available to belong to someone. Active and passive are divided between the possessor and the possessed, the lover and the beloved, for example. With that, we no longer have two subjects in a loving relationship.

The "to" is an attempt to avoid falling back into the horizon of the reduction of the subject to the object, to an item of property.

But how can a subject attach him or herself or be attached to another on a long-term basis? How can we prevent the length of this attachment from being dependent upon the judgment of a God-the-Father or King, upon the decisions of a civil authority, upon a genealogical kind of power or knowledge—whether dictated or elected? And how can the relationship between the lovers be saved from alienation through the family?

It could be that, behind the sacramental or juridical mirages of "Thou art mine," and I am thine, forever, there lies something natural, unresolved, which is projected onto the celestial or the law.

In my view, *I love to you* cannot be temporalized in this fashion: I love to you your natural subsistence, even if this "to" does not imply the sacrifice of the latter. For can what I love turn out to be obedience to a nature?

In our culture, this is still the fate that befalls the definition and condition of women, and those of men, too, insofar as he has to be a citizen whose nature is neutralized, as he also has to be the "head" for human kind (and for woman particularly), as well as the "image" of

~

divinity. All of this is to be expected with the lack of a culture of sexuality.

But am I able to love subjection to a nature, be it animal, human, or divine? Isn't freedom of movement lacking on both sides, a movement that constructs the one and the other and enables a common temporality to be constituted? If I am attentive to your intentionality, to your fidelity to yourself and to its/your becoming, then it is permissible for me to imagine whether there can be anything long-lasting between us, whether our intentionalities can come into accordance.

These intentionalities cannot be reduced to *one*. It is not enough to look ahead in the same direction, as Saint-Exupéry says, or even to ally rather than abolish differences. Man and woman, faithful to their identity, do not have the same intentionality, as they are not of the same gender, and do not occupy the same genealogical position. But they can make commitments to act together according to terms of agreement that render their intentionalities compatible: to build a culture of sexuality together, for example, or to construct a politics of difference.

In realizing our intentionality, each one of us can find support from alliances such as these.

And so: you do not know me, but you know something of my appearance. You can also perceive the directions and dimensions of my intentionality. You cannot know who I am but you can help me to be by perceiving that in me which escapes me, my fidelity or infidelity to myself. In this way you can help me get away from inertia, tautology, repetition, or even from errancy, from error. You can help me become while remaining myself.

Nothing here, then, suggests marriage through a contract that snatches me away from one family to chain me to another, nothing subjects me like a disciple to a master, nothing takes away my virginity, or halts my becoming within submission to another (supported by an Other or the State); nor is there anything to force my nature to reproduce. What we are dealing with, rather, is a new stage in my existence, one enabling me to accomplish my gender in a specific identity, related to my history and to a period of History.

For the generic universal is not transhistorical. It is to be hoped that it will be realized progressively, and, by extension, that this occurs throughout the world. It is now possible for the culture of sexual difference to spread throughout different peoples and traditions. Such an extension should be accompanied by (qualitative) progress, by a progressive distancing from animality and from the subjection of sexuality to reproduction or pornography.

This progress needs language. Not just the language of information, as I have suggested, but the language of communication, too. What we particularly need is a syntax of communication. For communication amounts to establishing links, and that is a matter for syntax.

Thus: how am I to speak to you? And: how am I to listen to you?

Note
  1. See note 3, p. 102. (Tr.)

~ II ~

In Almost Absolute Silence

Let us begin with: how am I to listen to you?

No longer is it a matter of listening to a message in terms of a content that has already been coded by society or language. Of course, that is always useful. If you let me know what time you are arriving or calling, it is useful for me to understand so that I am there when you do. If you tell me where we are to meet, I need to understand you in order to get there. And if you would like some fruit and I bring you a book, you will feel that I do not understand you.

Yet, this sort of communication is not enough to weave a web of alliances and histories between two subjects.

But expressing subjective affect will not manage it, either. For I can console your sadness but sadness is not necessarily what you intended and it does not necessarily help me in my own becoming. It is possible that your/my joy or your/my sadness could be a sign, an indication of the elaboration of our becoming, but this is rarely the case. And should either one of us submit to the other's pathos, it may well be that spirituality will not be formed in the relationship but elsewhere. Sentiment will bind one to the other, often in one direction and not reciprocally, and the locus of thought will be taken up by other realities and truths. This is often how it is in our civilizations, where thought is separated from affect, thought being a logical construction for truths beyond earthly contingencies, which are associated more with affects, with nature. In that case, marriage becomes a tale of love subjugated to faith in God or to the service of the State through the institution of the family and reproduction.

Thus, *I am listening to you* is not to expect or hear some information from you, nor is it the pure expression of sentiment (a rather naive aim of psychoanalysis sometimes). *I am listening to you* is to listen to your words as something unique, irreducible, especially to my own, as something new, as yet unknown. It is to understand and hear them as the manifestation of an intention, of human and spiritual development.

In relationships within genealogies, be they human or divine, natural or spiritual, the elder is supposed to know what the younger is and what he or she must become. The elder is supposed to know the younger, and only listens to him or her within the parameters of an existing science or truth. To attain sexual difference, to attain horizontality in transcendence, requires: I do not know you, hence the birth of solitude and respect for the mystery of the other. I comprehend you, I know you, often express the impossibility of attaining solitude. I alienate myself and I alienate you to/in a pseudo-reality or truth. I reduce you to my existence, to my experience, to what I already know so as to avoid solitude.

This sort of language is often used by adults, thus paralyzing the freedom of the child's becoming out of a lack of autonomy on the part of adults themselves.

I am listening to you, as to another who transcends me, requires a transition to a new dimension. I am listening to you: I perceive what you are saying, I am attentive to it, I am attempting to understand and hear your intention. Which does not mean: I comprehend you, I know you, so I do not need to listen to you and I can even plan a future for you. No, I am listening to you as someone and something I do not know yet, on the basis of a freedom and an openness put aside for this moment. I am listening to you: I encourage something unexpected to emerge, some becoming, some growth, some new dawn, perhaps. I am listening to you prepares the way for the not-yet-coded, for silence, for a space for existence, initiative, free intentionality, and support for your becoming.

I am listening to you not on the basis of what I know, I feel, I already am, nor in terms of what the world and language already are, thus in a formalistic manner, so to speak. I am listening to you rather as the revelation of a truth that has yet to manifest itself—yours and that of the world revealed through and by you. I give you a silence in which your future—and perhaps my own, but *with* you and not *as* you and *without* you—may emerge and lay its foundation.

This is not a hostile or restrictive silence. It is openness that nothing or no one occupies, or preoccupies—no language, no world, no God.

This silence is space-time offered to you with no a priori, no pre-established truth or ritual. To you it constitutes an overture, to the other who is not and never will be mine. It is a silence made possible by the fact that neither *I* nor *you* are everything, that each of us is limited, marked by the negative, non-hierarchically different. A silence that is the primary gesture of *I love to you*. Without it, the "to," such as I understand it, is impossible.

This silence is the condition for a possible respect for myself and for the other within our respective limits. It also assumes that the already existing world, even in its philosophical or religious form, should not be considered complete, already revealed or made manifest. If I am to be quiet and listen, listen to you, without presupposition, without making hidden demands—on you or myself—the world must not be sealed already, it must still be open, the future not determined by the past. If I am to really listen to you, all these conditions are essential. And moreover, that I do not consider language to be immutable. Otherwise, language itself controls, orders, and hinders freedom.

Of course, language is important. This third term or reality is always there between us. And claiming to reduce it to an immediate relation between the sexes is a naive move. But saying that a man speaks differently to a woman than a woman to a man is also problematic if language itself is not analyzed.[1] Language exists between us but is more modifiable than our difference. Many seem inclined to think the opposite, owing to speculative or religious idealism, social conformism, submission to some past that has the force of law, or being in the grip of the language of the father, or of ancestors, which it is deemed right to submit to or believe in.

Listening to you assumes that, for a moment at least, I may put all these obligations to one side. That no one or nothing forces any obligation upon me, no matter what my body, my lethargy, my tiredness might be telling me.

Listening to you thus requires that I make myself available, that I be once more and always capable of silence. To a certain extent this gesture frees me, too. But above all, it gives you a silent space in which to manifest yourself. It makes available to you a still virgin space-time for your appearance and its expressions. It offers you the possibility of existing, of expressing your intention, your intentionality, without you calling out for it and even without asking, without overcoming, without annulling, without killing.

I could list other processes that linguists, philosophy and psychoanalysis claim are necessary for communication. These processes never really give thought to one *with* the other in the serenity and the occasion of *being with*, respecting difference. They remain within the horizon of a single subject—more or less realized or fulfilled—in the horizon of the same, in the order of genealogy, of hierarchy. The *you* is then the same as *me*, more perfect, older, or the opposite. It is still a passage to the limit or beyond: the divine *Thou* of philosophers like Buber, the *Thou* of the Our Father. The *Thou* that is ecstatic but fundamentally the same as I, my superior equal, my remains on high, the fabricated transcendence with which I dialogue as with a sort of spiritual placenta, expecting to become greater or more perfect, to be born into difference.

This *Thou* traps in its mystery the irreducibility of the other, he or she who is horizontally transcendent to me. To relate to *he* or *she* via the detour of this *Thou* is indeed to subject difference to sameness and similarity, in the name of an ecstatic model outside the judgment of consciousness, thus to remain unaware of the lack of ethics in this gesture. The *Thou* of the wholly other with whom I dialogue, that other me, cannot be substituted for the mystery of the other of sexual difference, and I cannot subordinate this difference to *Him*.

It would be more correct, then, to refer oneself to *He* or *She*, the ideal representations of my own and the other gender's becoming. Yet it is true that the child is always within us, and that we need *you* as we need parental guidance. Therefore *you* cannot be only *you-father* at the risk of depriving the child I am of the warmest and most vital childhood guidance: *you-mommy*.

Once beyond this moment of intimacy with the child I am, it is towards the other that I should turn and, moreover, return trying not to impose on him or her any genealogical refuge or authority I may have.

You, who are you? You who are not nor ever will be me or mine.

Note

1. See, for example, some interesting commentaries that yet require a degree of modification in "*Discours sexué et intersexué*" in *Sexes et genres à travers les langues*, op. cit.

~ 12 ~

A Breath that Touches in Words

Listening to the other, sparing them some silent time, is respecting his or her breath, too. Only a mother breathes for her child. Once born, we all must, should, breathe for ourselves.

For this to be so, the relations between breathing and other acts, including speech, have to be reconsidered. Breathing and speaking use breath in almost inverse proportion, at least in our tradition, at least for most of us. Usually, our language, the language we use, our dialogues and exchanges, stifle breath more than they cultivate it. Our messages, our truths are generally breathless, suffocated and suffocating. The ideals we are presented with act like a sort of drug promising us ecstasy beyond ourselves. As if the less we breathe, the nearer we come to correct thinking. Death would then be the guarantee of our nearness to truth. And one only has to enter most of our public places, particularly religious ones, to see that scant attention is paid to the need for ventilation. Yet the (holy) spirit supposedly comes of breath. What is said is thus the opposite of or bears no relation to what is really practiced, except by a few people. Speech, instead of bearing breath, takes its place, replaces it, which invariably stifles and preoccupies the place for silence. People who pay no heed to respiration, who breathe poorly, who are short of air, often cannot stop speaking, and are thus unable to listen. Speaking is their way of respiring, or more precisely expiring, of exhaling, in order to take a breath. And so they stifle the inspiration—in the strict sense, general or figurative—of others, even those who take bodily and spiritual care of their breath.

It is, therefore, important to reflect upon the fact that a language, spirituality or religion that is founded on speech, yet pays no need to the silence and breath making it possible, might well lead to a lack of respect for life; for one's own life, for the other's life, for others' lives. Using breath and the body to define or pronounce something in quite certain terms, to structure a religion or a sociological symbolic order, becomes destructive when this bearer of life is not recognized or regenerated. Cultural practices constituted in this manner soon become authoritarian as a result of immobilizing and stifling breath. By forgetting the gift that comes from the living world (particularly the vegetable world), and human bodies (particularly female bodies), they become dogmatic. Such traditions substitute words for life without forging the necessary links between the two. Yet these links would be what enables life and language to be reciprocally preserved, regenerated and fecundated, especially in dialogue where breath can either be awakened, engendered, or stifled. In the transition from those traditions which respect breath to one subordinate(d) to speech, to the Word, heedless of breath, the manner of speaking has changed from poetic telling, hymns and chants, prayers of praise, and dialogue into pre-written discourses or texts, often resorting to the imperative, addressing the individual in his or her relation to the social group and not to cosmic reality nor to the other. The explicit or implicit model of the individual is, then, the male of the species determined by his human or divine genealogy, subjugated to the authority of oft absent gods of his own gender.

In this patriarchal type of horizon, the very use of words, the circulation of breath in and through language, has therefore changed.

Language is given over to ritual, repetition, a secondary attribution of values, speculation, and to a logic unsuited to life and its breath. It has been uprooted from its engendering in the present, from its connections with the energy of my own and the other's body, and with that of the surrounding natural world. And so writing a poem, singing a song of praise, as well as asking a question, sometimes making a request—of nature, of a lover, of a divinity we incarnate or could incarnate—is not to use breath in the same way as in following a prepared speech or text which expresses orders, laws or imperative truths rather than praises, thanks, or questions. With the former, we approach humans or divinities who watch over life, who respect and cultivate it. We are those men and women, humans, or gods, male and female, who protect life, who engender it or let it unfold; we are forever attuned to the cosmic world, to our corporeal nature, and not simply the product of a people or society; we are still alive and not merely fabricated or alienated within this fabrication for want of a possible return in/to ourselves. Without being conscious of it, we transform our vital respiration into spiritual breath. Nature becomes spirit while remaining nature.

That is how I interpret the myths to do with the birth of Buddha or the birth of the son of God, particularly the mystery of the Annunciation. In my view, respecting Mary's virginity does not mean forcing a Father-logos upon her whose son she conceives outside of her female body, as is all too often taught; rather, it means not touching her body without asking her if it is what she wishes or desires. What we celebrate in the name of the Annunciation would then be the time of shared words between a man and a woman prior to any carnal act or conception. Religious doctrines often transmit the opposite of what I take the moment of the Annunciation to teach us. They speak of submission and compulsion without the exchange of words.

Yet it is respect for speech, not in the form of imperatives but in dialogues between woman and man, that makes breath pass from the physiological centers of elemental vitality—the *chakras* of the stomach—to those of the heart, of speech, of thought. This movement is effected through the mediation of breath converged in speech.

The announcement to Mary is presented to us as a descending theology: God-the-Father sends a messenger to inform Mary that she will conceive a son by Him. Such is the interpretation associated with the mythologies of patriarchal eras. It is possible to give it another interpretation—less rich in imagery, to be sure—but more ethical, closer to an ascending theology, traditionally in keeping with female religions. In this case, the Annunciation corresponds to shared words between lovers prior to the celebration of their marrying. The man would cease to be the head to the woman's body, Father-the-Logos would cease to be the seed fertilizing mother-nature. Man and woman breathe together, engender together, carnally and spiritually. Their alliance is flesh becoming word—the announcement, the question, the dialogue, the thanks, the poetry of the encounter, and word becoming flesh: love, child, and so on, dialectically, to infinity. For the Magnificat is the song of praise for the announcement become body and for the fecundity of words which gave rise to an engendering that is not only natural but spiritual, too.

In this perspective, the exchange of words supplants the imperative and the unanswered question (Do you love me? Who am I?). The logos becomes dialogic, the relationship between living women and men and not an ecstasy of truth in an idealized beyond. Men and women speak to one another, fecundate one another. And the announcement to Mary can be understood differently from the way it has been passed on to us: the man agrees to question the woman and to ask for her word, without compulsion or force. The Annunciation hence resumes the expectation of the *Song of Songs*, "Do not rouse her, do not disturb my love, until *she* is ready."[1]

With this sharing, the carnal act becomes an act of speech, speech that respects woman and man, and is mindful of silence and breath.

This speech also remains tactile. It does not serve to designate a reality, a truth, an object outside the body, nor is it subservient to possession, to the acquisition of a property exterior to it. Nor can it be reduced to the supposed appropriation of speech to itself, to an already coded truth. Any more than it is the exteriorization of a univocal sentiment. Speech serves the communicating between selves.

In communicating, then, *touching upon* intervenes, a touching which respects the other proffering him/her attentiveness, including carnal attentiveness.

~

This *touching upon* asks for silence. To allow the other to emerge, silence is necessary, a silence that breaks the contiguity of a *touching* everything, each and every man or woman.

This *touching upon* requires breath, the safeguard of the presence of life and of its temporalization in a becoming of self non-destructive to the other.

This *touching upon* needs attentiveness to the sensible qualities of speech, to voice tone, to the modulation and rhythm of discourse, to the semantic and phonic choice of words.

This *touching upon* does not take place without a syntax constituting or bringing about the relation with the other. It is a grammar which prefers the question to the imperative; it chooses predicates manifesting an intentionality compatible with that of the other; it privileges verbs expressing dialogue, doing together; it uses *to, between, with, together*, rather than transitive forms, which always risk reducing the other to an object.

The *touching upon* cannot be appropriation, capture, seduction—to me, toward me, in me—nor envelopment. Rather it is to be the other's awakening to him/her and a call to co-exist, to act together and dialogue.

The intention of the *touching upon* would not be to tear the other away from the intimacy or interiority of his/her own self, from his/her temporality, nor to make him/her fall back into the natural immediacy of simple touching. In this *touching upon*, there is nature and spirit, breath, sensibility, body and speech.

Rather its intention would be to draw the other to the site of communication *with*, the site of the heart and the still sensible word. Its aspiration would be to awaken the other to an exchange in which the word is born and remains between two bodies, maintaining them in themselves by respecting their differences and spiritualizing them without removing them from their flesh.

The relation between man and woman seems to be the one where language is most needed because they cannot be reduced to one another, which rules out any potential comprehension of the other by reducing him/her to an object or to the same-as-oneself. Speech is essential between a woman and a man, women and men, but it cannot replace *touching upon*. Speech cannot distinguish between those men and women it claims to draw together, unite, and bring to dialogue. Thus it is important for it to touch and not become the alienation of the tactile in possession, in the elaboration of a truth or a disincarnated beyond, in the production of an abstract and supposedly neuter discourse. Speech must stay as word and flesh, language and sensibility, at the same time.

With this speech, there ceases to be a division between sensibility and intelligence, and they are most certainly not hierarchically ordered to the benefit of speculation estranged from the properties of bodies. Speech is intelligible because it remains sensible, related to the qualities of sound, rhythm, and meaning in the world of the subject(s).

The opposition between activity and passivity no longer has any meaning. Communication *between* and reciprocity, as well as respect for one's own gender (never simply one's own since it is engendered and remains partially exterior to one's self), respect for the gender of the other, for listening and silence, require *touching upon* without reduction or seduction, the safeguard of the sensible....

The division between the imperative and the interrogative is overcome, especially the way it is divided between the genders. I order myself in terms of the question you ask me. With every obligation there remains a "?" which prevents it from becoming an authority to believe in and to declare allegiance to. No law is valid as an adequate representation of meaning that might unilaterally control a nature, a body.

The subject and his or her intentionality avoid solipsism. Teleology becomes bi-univocal (which does not mean equivocal). The subject addresses him or herself to a female or male addressee, but receives her/himself back and is defined by him or her. The *I* is also engendered on the basis of *you*, unless the *I* reduces *you* to the same, to his or her image, to his or her own ideal, a mirage or illusion.

Any possibility of simply mastering a plan, project, or action is thwarted. The subject does not produce meaning alone, does not realize a task alone, nor accomplish an undertaking all alone. However, it does not follow that interaction with another subject or other subjects has to be immediate; it can be mediated in various ways. I can be in a relation (whether of intention, assistance, or dependence) with a woman or a man who is not present, who never has been or never will be present. I can be determined by a man or a woman who is no longer here, by the historical relevance of what he or she says, or by their *oeuvre*, for example.

~

Interdependency between subjects is no longer reduced to questions of possessing, of exchanging or sharing objects, cash, or an already existing meaning. It is, rather, regulated by the constitution of subjectivity. The subject does not vest its own value in any form of property whatsoever. No longer is it objecthood, having or the cost of having that governs the becoming of a subject or subjects and the relation among them. They are engaged in a relationship from which they emerge altered, the objective being the accomplishment of their subjectivity while remaining faithful to their nature. This journey might correspond to what is described in some myths as an honorable quest. Yet it is no longer a question of looking for some thing, of appropriating a beloved, an ideal located outside the self. The path is an internal one, accompanied by that of a male or female other who keeps him or her self outside of me, while pointing the way for me all the same. Intention concerns becoming the matter we are, the transfiguration of our body, our gender, our history. We realize this operation between us here and now, without taking leave of either the earth or flesh, the places we inhabit. It requires the invention of a language that enables us to communicate and exchange while nevertheless retaining the properties and qualities of our nature.

With this singular and multiple engagement between subjects of different genders, the impersonality of *one*, and its authority associated with the undifferentiated or with the summoning of a so-called neutral energy, tend to disappear. *Man* is no longer a *one*, a sort of abstract equal-to-all individual whose generic and specific qualities are both concentrated in and abolished by the institution of the family. *Woman* comes out of the anonymity of the *one*, ceases being a potential substitute for another woman, an object for use and exchange whose properties and functions, both natural and abstract, are determined by the needs of a given society, of a cultural era and its commerce. The *community* ceases to present itself as potentially *one*. It is made up of real persons, women and men, and is organized in terms of and through the economy of their differences. The neuter of the loss or lack of identity is no more, except in infidelity to one's own gender. Which avoids the risk of group totalization in which individual responsibility is neglected or stifled. Collective energy is constantly modulated by the relations between woman and man, women and men, ranging from the height of sensibility to the height of spirituality. The possibility of a mass will being formed susceptible to manipulation at the hands of a leader, a power, or an ideology is counteracted at every stage.

There yet remains this theoretical question. The neuter is supposed to represent a neither-one-nor-the-other. Before that neither-one-nor-the-other can be signified, the one and the other must actually exist, two different identities have to be defined in a way other than as artificially opposed poles of a single human model. Even if the identity of each gender has yet to be exhaustively determined or accomplished, we must use as our basis two irreducible identities.

For is there really such a thing as the neuter? What is it? What could its content be? To what reality does the neuter in language correspond in our era? If it refers to no real whatsoever, what is the point of it? Is it to sustain the antagonism between two reals that do differ, to be sure, but are not in opposition to one another? To sustain the existence of language as an autonomous and arbitrary web of meaning parallel to life and its properties?

It would be better to designate and express what is before claiming to neutralize or create in ignorance of what is erased in these processes. Hence, there are girls and boys. What does the term "children" signify if not a restrictive way of expressing a mixed plural? Women and men exist. Why sacrifice their reality to belonging to an abstract human kind that remains ill-defined?

Note
1. *The New English Bible*, Oxford University Press, 1970.

~ 13 ~

Practical Teachings:
Love — Between Passion and Civility

At this time—of the globalization and universalization of culture—but when this globality and universality are now ungovernable and beyond our control, making us divided and torn between differing certainties, opinions, dreams or experiences, it seems appropriate to return to what is governable by us here and now: love.

How can "I love you" be said in a different way? This is one of the most pertinent questions of our time. We have learnt something about sharing bread, money, living conditions. We engage in a sort of generosity or charity towards our literal or figurative neighbor, the furthest away often valued more than the one nearby, the dead more honored than the living. We still do not know how to love ourselves with respect and in reciprocity here and now. Whether it is a question of our bodies or our words, we remain subject to the power or hierarchy of the one who possesses, of the one who has *more* or *less*—knowledge or sex as well as wealth—of the one who can give or make some *thing*, in an economy of relations (especially amorous ones) subordinate to the *object*, to *objects*, to *having*. We know practically nothing about sharing between ourselves as persons, about the sharing of love between two persons. The transition from one stage of individual and collective History to another still needs to be realized by us.

The foundation for this cultural (r)evolution, its most radical locus, lies in the changing relations between man and woman, men and women.

How can we say, "I love you" differently? In order to answer this question with respect to existing reality, I carried out some research into the way women and men speak, and further research into their discourses, their dreams and their experiences regarding love. I did this with the help of colleagues who speak various languages, who belong to different cultures and religions. Those questioned were of various ages and socio-cultural backgrounds.

There were many differences between the responses given by women and men, differences that partly explain their attraction for one another, yet also explain the difficulties they find in realizing their desire for one another, their union with one another.

In this book I have focused on one of these differences in particular: women privilege relations between subjects while men give priority to relations to the object.

And so, in the words, whether real or imaginary, that the little girl addresses to her mother, there are always two persons speaking to one another and they are represented as doing something together. Rarely is there an object circulating between them, except an object of communication. The little girl shows her mother a loving intention, an ethical one, as it were. She sets up a just and communicative micro-society between her mother and herself. This community takes place between two women, one young, the other older, a minor and an adult. Unfortunately, the mother does not show the same intersubjective respect for her daughter. While they remain two, they no longer have the same right to speak. The mother commands, the daughter is to listen and obey. The elder seems to repeat to her daughter what has been forced upon her as a woman. A dominant male culture has intervened

~

between mother and daughter and broken off a loving and symbolic exchange. The position of the man relative to the object has separated the two women subjects. The message between them has become the imperative of an action to be accomplished and not a question that allows the other to speak. Another reason for the quasi-inversion of the daughter's intention in the mother's discourse could be the privilege attributed to *he/they (il(s))* over *she/they (elle(s))*, which devalorizes the daughter relative to the son, whom the mother addresses in a different way. The still common practice of reducing the woman to motherhood also leaves her without any cultural mediations to help her relate to her gender.

And yet young girls still dream of accomplishing intersubjective communication. They dream of sharing carnal and spiritual love with a male lover (or first of all with a female lover, in some cases). They dream of the communion of body and spirit, of exchanging words and social activities. Interestingly, they dream of sharing love with a partner more than they dream of motherhood. For them a child is the fruit of love *with*, and not of *having*.

Thus, little girls speak lovingly and socially, adolescent girls dream of sharing love. Little girls and adolescent girls reveal a desire for intersubjective relations: of life *with*.

Little boys talk mostly about possessing objects, and then about ideas; adolescent boys dream of erotic, romantic or social exploits, but not of sharing between persons. Which explains the widespread notion of the need for an objectival elaboration against the desire for incestuous regression.

How can we build bridges between two such different identities? This task requires cultural and juridical changes. The latter seem most pressing as changes in custom require more time to take effect.

In order to love, there have to be two persons. The person is defined by a civil identity. But there is no definition of woman as woman in the French Civil Code, nor one for the man as a man, for that matter. In love, then, man and woman are not defined as sexed identities but as neuter individuals—actually non-existent—or as instinctual and reproductive nature.

If we are to keep faith with the sexual liberations which have taken place and the changes in political horizon they have brought about, and if we are to enable cultural cohabitation between us, whether here or elsewhere, we must grant women and men rights corresponding to the reality of their respective needs.

For woman, there are at least four of these rights:

— the right to physical and moral inviolability, that is, to a civil identity guaranteed by a positive law which does not force each woman to defend herself in each case only via the criminal justice system against rape (which is considered as a crime and not as rape), battery, incest, pornography, involuntary prostitution, particularly in the public use of representations of women's body and speech;

— the right to voluntary motherhood without Church or state leaders exercising, either directly or through institutions, real power over a woman, and that includes financial or ideological power;

— the right to culture, that is, to languages, religions, sciences, and arts appropriate to female identity;

— a preferential and reciprocal right for mother and child(ren), particularly as a guarantee against violence and economic poverty, but also to assist mothers and children in inter-cultural marriages which lack suitable legislation.

In the absence of such a legislative framework, woman remains subject to a familial and conjugal institution in which she enjoys no rights as a woman; nor do lovers. The existing marriage contract is defined in terms of the married couple's material survival, and in terms of reproduction and raising children, and acquiring and possessing property, which is still always assumed to be principally the man-father's (the woman only has the right to property or capital if she is able to equal herself to the man, that is, in countries where such legislation does exist and subject to its application).

The legal age of marriage in the French Civil Code attests to this: for one, there is civil majority, for the other natural maturity, related to reproduction. Even if there are some exceptions to this rule in the law of neighboring countries, this is generally the case. The fact that the girl as a minor becomes an adult "through marriage" manifests yet again the female gender's subjection to existing institutions and customs rather than the girl's civil recognition as an autonomous person.

Therefore, the law has to be changed for love. So that lovers remain two in love, woman and man have to be civil adults and their alliance has to be guaranteed by words that have a value for both of them.

As far as civil law is concerned, and indeed the whole of culture, it is thus a matter of thinking somewhat less in terms of having and somewhat more in terms of being, the safeguard of being resting in the recognition of the existence of two different humans: man and woman.

It would be advantageous if the juridical transformations were to come about quickly in order to give us time to alter our customs and norms. Changes would aim towards giving the citizens who make up civil society a real identity, rather than defining them in relation to the private or public ownership of property.

If we are to intervene in the evolution of culture, particularly in the relations between love and speech, there are two initiatives we can take at any given moment to counteract our entrenched customs: we can change our way of speaking and communicating, and transform our way of loving.

Each and every woman and man can be attentive to recognizing the other as an irreducible source of meaning. We can allow women to have their say as much as men do, and ensure that we enable or give preference to exchanges between *I* and *you* as sexed. We can say *she/they* (*elle(s)*) as many times as *he/they* (*il/(s)*), whether we are women or men, which would attribute an objective representation of equivalent value to I_{she} and I_{he}, *you*$_{she}$ and *you*$_{he}$. While women may have learned to say *I* at times—or have remained at the *I* stage in this culture of ours?— they barely use *she/they* (*elle(s)*) to designate themselves and to designate other women. Then the *you* and *we* often become, for these women, a *you*$_{he}$, *him* or *them*$_{he}$. The deliberate use of *she/they* alters our customs without our being aware of it and enables the relations between the sexes and their representations through gender to be subject to a dialectic. We can also take account of women's speech in the same way as we do men's, whether it is a question of signification, truth, or beauty, and given this fact, continue to elaborate a meaning that respects two different identities. In short we can, to give just a few examples, endeavor

~

to give preference to the exchange of speech and listening between us without making objects or possessions a priority; we can seek to establish being-together in preference to rivalries over having.

We can also attempt, day by day, to change our ideals and our teaching concerning love. Within the horizon of theories of sexuality, Freudian or Lacanian ones, for instance, the father is always the legislator; libido is described as instinctual andmasculine, at best neuter; it is assumed that desire must remain foreign to love; adult sexuality is determined by reproduction and not through the relation of male and female genders.

These theories may be knowledgeable but they do not offer us a culture of sexuality. They describe and perpetuate an absence of culture.

This goes hand in hand with a jurisdiction that is inadequate at the level of the individual: institutions tied to familial and patriarchal authority under which everyone alienates a part of his or her identity; citizens poorly determined by being defined as masculine-neuter; property ownership taking precedence over the consideration of persons and their rights and obligations as persons; confusion between the civil, the military and the religious, and a lack of civil rights and duties for women as well as, more generally, for individuals as sexed.

Now one of the perils of our culture stems from women's loss of identity, either through reducing them to nature, to man's object or property, or through the female gender's identification with man. To become man in the fullest sense is still not to become a woman. It is to lose generic identity, which does nothing to resolve the problems faced by individuals, couples, and a sexed human society. Nor does this solution accord with the components of each person's identity, engendered as he or she is by woman and man.

Women's collusion with the between-men society leads, moreover, to an increasingly impoverished and sexist sexuality. Desire manifests itself as quasi-mechanistic forces, functioning with no sensorial, sensual pleasure. Woman, assumed to have no libido of her own, devotes her energy to exacerbating, an's sexual tension, for which she becomes the site of discharge. In these abstract, stifling, disenchanted, not to say cynical, physical encounters, procreation remains the only tangible symptom of the existence of life and sensibility. Hence its value.

A return to the origins of our culture shows that this was not always the case, that there was an era in which it was the woman who initiated love. At that time, woman was goddess and not servant, and she watched over the carnal and spiritual dimension of love. In her, love and desire were indivisible. The goddess's principal attribute was tenderness, not a quality denoting a universal goodness directed towards all beings but rather a differentiated sentiment vis-à-vis the other gender, being brought to bear in the carnal act itself. According to our mythology, it is Aphrodite who represents the first figure of love incarnated in a human body, love that is not chaotic, without measure, without rhythm or temporality, a simply cosmic, pure and incestuous love.[1] Consequently, attaining a sexed identity does not derive from the paternal prohibition of incest but from the realization of the desire between woman and man with each being respected, and from their membership of the human species.

According to our Western tradition, sexual chaos reigned both prior to and after Aphrodite, and one of the reasons for the regression appears to be the man-father's seizure of power which is linked to the man-lover's incapacity to differentiate himself from the mother, who is once again assimilated to a nature without consciousness. The incest taboo decreed by the father has not stopped man from returning to chaotic drives, whereby the energy accumulated in being estranged from the woman-mother is then expended without measure and without sharing. The obligation to reproduce figures as the remedy for death and for the return to indifferentiation, imagined as a prenatal situation in which there is a state of fusion with the mother. The only realities likely to help man not to sacrifice himself entirely to eros seem to be procreation and forming a family, aside from labor and the acquisition of family capital, which in our culture appear as forms of punishment or redemption with regard to the vicissitudes of the flesh or the possibility of a for-itself corresponding to the marriage contract between the married couple.

In this perspective, the relation between the genders is determined by man's needs with no consideration for woman's identity, which consists more of the desire for and with another—woman or man. Woman, who is born of the same as herself, is far less familiar with this nostalgia for regression into the mother; for her it is artificial.

The girl feels desire for relations with her mother, a desire then transferred almost exclusively to the man for both good and bad reasons, as our tradition lacks the mediations enabling her to keep her identity as a woman. As I have already suggested, it is moving to observe that the most intersubjective language is produced by the little girl in her relation with her mother, the reverse not being true. It is from a desire for exchange that women's melancholy ensues rather than from nostalgia for return, particularly for a regression to undifferentiated nature.

However, given the prevalence of *one* genealogy, a patriarchal one, female filiation is erased, and while the wife (of a son) becomes mother (of a son), the father's virgin daughter, by virtue of her status as such, becomes a currency among men. Justice would mean woman's being virgin and mother for herself, these properties of her nature founding her spiritual becoming, her rights and duties, instead of her being reduced to an elementary naturalism in which virginity is equated with the presence of the hymen, and maternity with the fact of having actually given birth. Is it not true that even today religious and State institutions still actually consider woman to be the natural body of which man remains the spiritual head, whether he is head of the church, head of state, or head of a family?

In such an economy, intersubjective relations between the genders are lacking in maturity, particularly sexual maturity. Man and woman do not consider themselves as two people with a different identity. And they marry or come together on the basis of contracts concerned with having: food, shelter, goods, children, etc. Restricting ourselves to civil undertakings of this kind exposes, among other things, existing prohibitions and prudishness regarding the sexual domain. But legal formulations such as these do not encourage the realization of subjective interiority. The demand for equal rights, particularly legal rights, might itself be a regressive step in the definition of an identity proper to each gender.

In fact, there is still an absence of a culture of sexuality, of flesh, of generic identity.

We are between: love (it goes without saying, the less we talk about it, the better it is), and a system of taboos weighing heavily upon the relations between the sexes. Which love are we talking about, then?

The approach of Far-Eastern traditions, especially the practice of yoga, coupled with the philosophical meditation inseparable from it, has taught me another way, a way leading not to a discharge but to an energetic recharge, to a regeneration and a culture of energy. In concrete terms that means, as I suggested in the *Introduction*, that in our bodies, there are energetic centers, *chakras*, situated at the crossroads of various physiological and spiritual functions. Traditionally, the arousal and the circulation of energy through these conduits are linked to the elemental states of matter—earth, water, fire, air, ether—to which there are corresponding densities, forms, colors, syllables, divinities, and specific cardinal points.

And so, "in the body of the believer, that part of the body between the feet and the knees is related to the Earth element; Earth is square and yellow in color; it is symbolized by the syllable Lam; the circulation of breath in this area of the body is accompanied by meditation upon Brahma, the golden-colored god...."[2]

The person following these techniques will endeavor to bring the different *chakras* of his/her body and the dimensions of the universe into relation with one another by appropriate postures and gestures, by mastering breathing, visualizing forms and colors, and emitting sounds. Such a knowledge of energy is gained thanks to the preferably oral teaching of an experienced practitioner. The spiritualization of nature, be it micro- or macrocosmic, is associated with the worship of divinities, guardians of certain parts of the body and the world; divinities themselves always subordinate to becoming and to the incarnation of energy. It may be realized by the renunciation of carnal desire between the sexes, an option quite similar to Western monasticism except that the place for retreat is the forest or mountain rather than a cloister; hermitism is preferred over community life and chastity is chosen after a fulfilled erotic life.

Indeed, this is often expressed in those texts which disclose the worship of a Goddess (worship of her body and her sex) by man. But there is nothing to stop knowledge of energy from becoming the vehicle for a carnal and spiritual relation between man and woman, a dual and

~

reciprocal relation, in which the genders are united as micro- and macrocosmic humanity.

Love between man and woman thus becomes the mastery and culture of energy rather than its instinctual expenditure, to be redeemed by procreation here on earth and faith in asexual happiness in the beyond—the path to this being the acquisition of an insensible *logos*. The carnal act ceases to be a regression to degree zero for pleasure or words; rather it is the locus for the lovers' revival and becoming. Love is accomplished by two, without dividing roles between the beloved and the lover, between objectival or animal passivity on the one hand, and generally conscious and valorous activity on the other. Woman and man remain two in love. Watching over and creating the universe is their primary task, and it remains so.

Such a cultivation of relationships between the genders can be transposed into community relations. Instead of seducing (one another) to expend (one another's) energy, man and woman, woman and man contribute, one another alike, one to the other, what it takes to cultivate their desire for one another.

Given this perspective, the way women and men come together is transformed.

No longer do men and women approach one another without the *words* of them both. These words are such that they leave two persons an identity. For example, *I love you* risks reducing the other to the object of my love. This way of speaking should be used with caution. It would be better to say: *I love to you*, or in you I love that which both is and becomes, that which is forever foreign to me. *I desire you* poses an even greater threat to an intersubjective relation than *I love you*.

Other words exist which are better at respecting the two subjects who come together:

I hail you	I praise you
I thank you	I celebrate you
I ask you	I bless you, etc.
I offer you	

These words generally involve two persons, and the participation of the two in a relation, in reciprocity. Here the secret vector would always be: *Who are you?*

This question would remain latent between man and woman, irreducible as they are to one another. Of course, no one can be reduced to anyone else, but the most fundamental locus of irreducibility is between man and woman. To make one or the other your property or similar to you, is to remove the question: *Who are you?*, a question that maintains their development and the relation between the two.

Thus, love and desire would always be questioning and in the process of becoming. Whom do I love? And who am I to love? Who am *I*? Who are *you*?

In cultures where sexual attraction is cultivated, certain *gestures* express the desire for coming together, for union.

A greeting is made by the whole body.

A request for carnal union may be expressed by the hands.

Hands are placed in different positions depending on the degree of union desired.

These modalities of speech and gesture can be brought into relation with:

forms
colors
sounds
fragrances
breath

appropriate to man and to woman and to each of their *chakras*.

Love, even carnal love, is therefore cultivated and made divine. The act of love becomes the transubstantiation of the self and his or her lover into a spiritual body. It is a feast, celebration, and a renaissance, not a decline, a fall to be redeemed by procreation. Love is redemption of the flesh through the transfiguration of desire *for* the other (as an object?) into desire *with* the other.

What is remarkable in these traditions is the fact that thought is ready to listen to nature, to the sensible. The famous example of this is Buddha contemplating a flower. For him, this gesture probably represents the perfect act, since it respects nature while becoming spiritual. The overcoming of matter by spirit—the privileging of the speculative over the sensible is, therefore, no more. Buddha becomes spirit while remaining sensible, awakened flesh. Surely this is a fine lesson in love?

We may be given a further lesson in love through a non-patriarchal interpretation of the Annunciation, taken as a symbol of the relations between the sexes.

The Annunciation is given the following rather univocal interpretation nowadays: Mary, you who are young and still a virgin, thus beautiful and desirable, the Lord, who has power over you, is informing you through his messenger that he wishes to be the father of a son to whom you will give birth. Mary can only say "yes" to this announcement because she is the Lord's possession or his property. The mystery of the angel remains.

There is another possible interpretation: Mary, you who, from adolescence, are divine, because you were born of a woman faithful to herself—Anne, the one said to have conceived without sin—you who are thus capable of intersubjectivity, the expression of love between humans, do you want to be my lover and for us to have a child together, since I find you worthy of this even though you are young, inexperienced and without any possessions. It is only thanks to your *yes* that my love and my son may be redemptive. Without your word, we may not be carnally redeemed or saved.

Such an interpretation of the Annunciation, which is how I now view it, is supported by the tradition of the physical and spiritual centers of the body, the *chakras*.

And so, in the iconography:

> words coming from the sky,
> the ray of sunlight,
> the song of the bird,
> the hands of Mary (and sometimes those of the Angel)

touch and designate the body between heart, breath and word, instead of announcing a spiritual conception.

In other words, the Lord does not take Mary without having exchanged with her in the place where word and flesh fecundate one another intentionally. Words and listening shared voluntarily between the lovers enable a divine child to be conceived. This conception is preceded by the transition from an almost undifferentiated corporeal matter, and from a separation between the genders, to an alliance in the word between man and woman. The announcement of the child's coming or incarnation is represented by angels in our tradition, angels who are messengers from the Lord and the cosmic realm.

In the Indian tradition, the bird is often the one to assist in the birth of life or in its safeguarding, and then in the acquisition of wisdom. It is a bird that helps Vishnu, the creator, as well as Brahmin, and every postulant of spiritual becoming. The bird accompanies the god with his body as a support for his movement in space, and then with his questions. The assistance of the bird comes closer and closer to speech. In interpersonal relations, the divine messenger is an angel, able to walk while keeping his wings, symbols of a harmonious relation with the air, with breath, whether it is a question of movement, of breathing, or of speaking.

The announcement to Mary can thus be interpreted as questions addressed to her in the form of speech, a question asking if she agrees to become the lover of the Lord and mother of his son. That question (which is incomplete, of course, since it principally concerns conception—the conception of a son moreover; it is also elliptical in that it situates Mary's speech as what separates Father and Son without stating this explicitly) is to be understood as the announcement of the spiritual assumption of Mary thanks to a Lord capable of knowing his own desire, of interiorizing it and sharing it in word and flesh.

This Lord would then be a figure surpassing or accomplishing Buddha: the awakened one who is compassionate, agrees to speak, love, and engender in order to redeem, as a couple, the whole of the macro- and microcosmic universe. With this gesture the Lord actually renounces having, the object, power, in order to accede to being-man and to the realization of intersubjectivity with the being of woman, who is able to conquer or retain her virginity. And that alliance, a dual then communal alliance, could incarnate the finality of History, or at least lead the way to another era.

~

Notes

1. See "*Le mystère oublié des généalogies féminines,*" in *Le temps de la différénce,* op. cit. and *Le rôle d'Éros et d'Aphrodite dans les cosmogonies grecques,* Jean Rudhart, PUF, Collège de France, Essais et conférences, 1986.

2. Extract from the *Yogatattva Upanishad,* reprinted in *Upanishads du Yoga* (trans. Jean Varenne), Gallimard, Coll. Tel Unesco. See also *Kundalini, l'énergie des profondeurs,* Lilian Silburn, Les Deux Océans, Paris, 1983. My translation. (Tr.)

~ EPILOGUE ~

An encounter between a woman and a man may reach a dimension of universality if it takes place with each being faithful to their gender. Such an event reveals a fault-line in the construction of History, and lays bare the horizon of a new era to be built both actively and consciously.

We have, in fact, yet to see a true democratic control of life and culture by all men and women. The revelation that neither nature nor the subject nor the absolute can be one, and that multiplicity is likely to lead to death, still needs to be brought to light. We still know nothing of the fecundity between a woman and a man, women and men. Having children is a natural act that does not mark a real limit between human kind and other species. And as we are not actually two, it would be claiming too much to say that we already have children in accordance with our will and spiritual desire. Besides, that is not enough to constitute us as men and women, but only as fathers and mothers.

We have a pressing need: to get away from the hold genealogy has over us in order to accomplish this task and responsibility in a different way. Conferring power on children seems a feeble demagogic measure, returning to God-the-Father a thinly disguised act of blind desperation. It remains for us to refound the relations between humans on the basis of the sovereignty of an unpower: being women or men.

Is not our task to cultivate this generic destiny as the fecundity of all relations, both public and private? And isn't this measure likely to further the *oeuvre* of our tradition while respecting it, especially Hegel's *oeuvre*? For such a labor to be effected, we can no longer simply invert a vertical structure; we have to confer transcendence upon horizontality. To recognize you, you-man, as transcendent to me, to uphold in nature and spirit the transcendence between us, women and men—wouldn't this be the way to attain another subjectivity, another alterity, another community, more real, concrete and human? Doesn't this also mean accepting that spirit is in each one of us, provided we are faithful to our self as a gender, and that we only experience one part of spirit, limited as we are to our generic identity?

The *oeuvre* of human incarnation thus becomes the locus for the dialectic's becoming. It is realized between nature and culture without forsaking one pole to the advantage of the other. At the subjective and objective level, it is accomplished thanks to the labor of and between *I* and *you*, *he* and *she*, I_{she} and you_{he}, I_{he} and you_{she}, each irreducible to the other, co-founders of nature and culture.

In such a perspective, my part of the universal is within me, and I do not have to go out of myself or renounce my nature in order to attain it. With generic identity, there is no longer an opposition between particular and universal in the sense that the universal is already within me and does not have to be constructed outside of me. Of course, I am still subject to a historical particularity. But no longer is there any contradiction between the singularity of that history and a neuter (?) universal produced by a culture, a spirit. That tension is resolved within the horizon of belonging to a universal as generic identity. I no longer have any reason to estrange myself from myself so as to meet up with the absolute in a for-itself existing outside of me. Rather, I have to realize myself as what and who I am: a woman. This woman I am has to realize the female as universal in the self and for the self as far as she is able during the period of History in which she finds herself and given the familial, cultural, or political contingencies she has to overcome.

For such a development of my gender, my subjectivity becomes objectivity while remaining subjectivity. The sensible interiority of my individual history has to overcome certain particularities in realizing my gender, that relatively abstract dimension of my destiny which must be internalized while remaining partially external to me inasmuch as it belongs to an engendered body and to a community of the same gender.

Concrete, irreducible, exteriority comes to me from the other gender, in relation to which my interiority constitutes itself in difference. I become woman in constructing the interiority, the spirit, the ideality of the gender I am. My gender remains partially exterior to me in that I belong to a historical community, of women particularly. It is not out of the question for me to distance myself from this in order to determine for myself and for others the universal of my gender since I am a woman. The irreducible criterion of exteriority hence lies in the existence of the other gender and that of nature. My interiority, then, can have no claims to the absolute nor to the infinite except in the horizon of one gender. But one gender does not correspond to the whole and can only be determined in respect for the other and for the universe as subsisting outside of me.

I thus differentiate myself within myself through the facts of my being a particular individual and of my belonging to a gender. This process enables me to make a pact with a person of the other gender without the mediation of the object. And that assumes a differentiation within him or herself as well. Such a differentiation within ourselves through fidelity to our gender opens up between us the space-time of a subjective and objective alliance based upon recognition, respective rights, love, culture.

The pact with a person of my own gender is paradoxically less straightforward due to the risk of objectivity dissipating into sameness and the danger of measuring (probably competitively) the gender's appropriateness to itself. Collective representations, rights, and ideals are needed that would enable us to constitute a sociality as a function of the intention of the gender as universal. This intention obviously cannot be determined by substituting the negation of the other gender for the labor of the negative vis-à-vis oneself. In other words, engaging with a person of my own gender is threatened with superficiality, dissolution, with an unethical sensibility as long as there are no just institutions appropriate to it.

That is not the case with a gender different from mine, not only because of natural attraction and reproduction, as generally thought, but more because of the creativity difference produces, and the energy engendered by the double labor of the negative transforming immediate impulse or absolute desire into a presence that is attentive and restrained, focused and available, open and reflective, reciprocal in fidelity to the self. It is thus that a new determination of intentionality takes place. It becomes possible for each to be engendered naturally and spiritually by the other, and with the other—with the past, present and future, particular and universal good being respected.

The double definition of the generic by a negative is not produced abstractly. It requires a man and a woman to come together and to represent an incarnation of their gender in the self, for the self and for the other. In other words, they have to mark a limit for one another in the claim to being, to knowing or wanting themselves to be the whole; they have to bring one another to the revelation of an ontic and ontological difference; they must offer assistance to one another in realizing their gender; for its simultaneously particular and universal destiny. Any contract between the two would suggest mutual assistance for the development of his and her gender, individually and collectively.

Such a coming together and such a pact end the ceaseless drifting of men and women and their alienation in property, in others, in constructs or theories of collectivity, of culture or of History. They represent the alliance of the natural and the spiritual, of exteriority and interiority, of the ontic and the ontological, of the particular and the universal. The purpose of such an alliance is not reproduction or the acquisition of property but the realization of flesh, spirit and History, in peace, felicity and fecundity.

The labor of love between man and woman cannot have for its natural or state-determined objective the founding of a family. Under no circumstances should "marriage" entail the loss of generic identity in a private or public institution. It is the engagement of two intentionalities to realize the finality of their gender.

The wedding between man and woman realizes the reign of spirit. Without it, there is no spirit. Any universal corresponding to a single gender or claiming to be neuter sins against spirit. And to sin against spirit is absolute. Everything else can be forgiven. Apart from that other infamy: destroying nature itself as the source of life for each and every man and woman.

Sinning against spirit can arise from infidelity to a proper identity or from depriving the other of the intentionality appropriate to his or her gender.

Aside from ensuring that each person accomplishes his or her destiny, we have to work towards a universal will. Now this is a function of two wills, and it is their alliance alone that might at times incarnate a universal dimension. For why doubt that man's intention does seek a good, a truth, a beauty? But he is a particular marked by his own nature, qualities, and history. His intention cannot claim to be the general one. And the whole of his tradition is marred by an original sin: to have mistaken the reason of man for the universal.

Neither his intention nor my own can be elevated to a concrete universal. Yet when his intention envisages this, and mine, too, as the good for all men and women, including ourselves, the meeting of our wills can reach a dimension of universality. It is particular, without a doubt, since it is historic and the expression of a specific culture, but it is general enough to incorporate the singularities and particularities of our time without suppression or opposition.

This meeting, this alliance even, of two intentions, each one faithful to its gender, assumes that we are renouncing what has previously been called the love between man and woman: instinctual or drive-related attraction in natural immediacy; the contract involving the traditional division of tasks (nature for me, public life for him); a make-do composition of our particularities by forsaking ourselves to the *laissez-faire* of History; the subjection of our sexed existences to an already existing culture, to its laws and civil and religious leaders; the priority significance accorded to natural and spiritual reproduction.

We cannot go along with any of that anymore. For what in former times appeared to be ethical nowadays proves to be mistaken, an abdication of responsibility, childish, the blind negation of belonging to a gender, a practice creating lies and injustice.

Respect for the negative, the play of the dialectic between us, would enable us to remain ourselves and to create an *oeuvre* with the other. And thus to develop, building a temporality instead of believing in eternal promises. We can construct a History on the basis of an interiority without power. We need to be two for this task, a man and a woman. Two indefinitely, weaving relations between nature and culture, the universe and society.

Determining and practicing relations of indirection between us, which enable us to respect ourselves and each other, form alliances, love ourselves and each other—as two or in the community—opens up the possibility for a fairer and better future. The relation between women and men thus renounces natural instinct. Flesh itself becomes spiritual while remaining flesh; affect becomes spirit while remaining love.

This alchemy needs measures, words, and ways which bring together while distancing, elevate while incarnating, individualize while universalizing. It implies a culture of breath, a becoming between earth, fire and water that overcomes inertia, submersion, ice, fire, and void, one where air subsists as indispensable matter for life and for its transubstantiation in spirit. This is a process which is, however, always uncertain within the truth of its operation. So returning to breath is the measure of respect for the self, for the other, for the living and its culture.

Air, that which brings us together and separates us. Which unites us and leaves a space for us between us. In which we love each other but which also belongs to the earth. Which at times we share in a few inspired words. Yet if the trees are unable to hear them, aren't they dead already? Air, the place in which to dwell, to cultivate flowers and angels. The place to await one another in life, whether outside or inside. In which to breathe and contemplate what unites and divides us, what connects us to the universe and makes our solitude and our exchanges possible. Universal matter of the living. The most necessary, most spiritual. Of which we are born and might on occasion engender. The element of our incarnation and our immortality. Of our passage from the nearest to the farthest, of our own identity and our alliance. Air, the future and return in which we become without ever being able to stop ourselves, or hardly ever. Air, which gives us forms from within and from without and in which I can give you forms if the words I address to you are truly destined for you and are still the *oeuvre* of my flesh.

To think you, to think of you. Love in thought, thought in love: the birth of spirit in us and between us.

To love to you and, in this "to," provide space for thought, for thought of you, of me, of us, of what brings us together and distances us, of the distance that enables us to become, of the spacing necessary for coming together, of the transubstantiation of energy, of the *oeuvre*.

To you: spacing in order to pass from affectivity to the spiritual, from interiority to exteriority. I see you, I hear you, I perceive you, I listen to you, I watch you, I am moved by you, astonished by you, I leave to breathe outside, I reflect with earth, water, stars, I think of you, I think you, I think of us: of two, of all men, all women, I begin to love, love to you, I return towards you, I try to speak, to tell to you: a feeling, a will, an intention, for now, for tomorrow, for a long time. I ask of you a place and time for today, for soon, for life, mine, yours, for the life of many.

The *to you* comes through breath trying to make itself speech. It seeks help from the outside, from thought, from History.

The *to you* enables expectation. It is not merely a present third term but a space of memory and birth. The *to you* is where we hold our own, engender, suspend already actualized action or truth. The *to you*: reminder of the mediations necessary for the construction of History.

And how am I to think you, remaining a virgin? To you? Air keeping the copula from hardening up or disappearing into is. "To" and not "is." To you, without appropriation, possession or loss of identity, with respect for distance. To you, other, man. Between us this "to," intention without object, cradle of being, whose shores are sexed.

Belonging to a gender seems to guarantee a dialectic of alterity and intersubjectivity. Such fidelity enables us to withdraw from each other (*se recueillir*) [?] and to meet each other, the limit upheld thanks to by difference from the other. The other, not the others or the same. The other, the irreducible, the one who remains without, forever unknown.

We try to hail ourselves, to give ourselves a sign. The one who touches brings joy. And how much must we love then to remain two!

~

But isn't this love at last? Love in the ideal? The bridge between the past and the future? The safeguard of life and time. The concentration and diffusion of an energy at work. Already formed but not accomplished, without final completion. Neither nature nor pure act, one and the other.

Beauty helps us discover a measure and direct the growth of relations between us. The dimension of love helps us to overcome immediate affect or attraction. It dwells while becoming, attracts while maintaining distance, allows for respect and contemplation. A sort of sun that illuminates in us and between us. Sometimes appearing in a gesture, a smile, a voice, a word, marks of a presence which approaches while distancing.

Without a doubt, we approached, maybe even passed by, one another. Your retreat reveals my existence, as my withdrawal is dedicated to you. May we come to recognize the intention here as a pathway leading indirectly to us.